Needle in a Haystack

by
Paula Agauas

Needle in a Haystack

All rights reserved. No part of this publication may be reproduced in any form, except for brief quotations in reviews, without the written permission of the publisher.

Published by:
Alan Koebel Jr.
Koebel Publishing
1632 Claxton Road
Dawson Springs, KY 42408-6906

First Edition: February, 1999
Second Edition: November, 2017

ISBN-13: 978-1978179356

ISBN-10: 1978179359

Table of Contents

Preface..4
Forward..5
Introduction..8
1. My Nightmare Begins..9
2. A Hiding Place...16
3. Guardian Angel...23
4. New Grandparents..27
5. Fortune Telling Resistance...............................33
6. Kidnapped...44
7. Sign Language...55
8. Foster Parents...61
9. Rubin...67
10. Jesus, the Messiah..70
11. Blind Eyes...81
12. The Holy Spirit...87
13. A Perfect Child..107
14. Vacation by Grace..111
15. A Place for Us..117
About the Author..121

Preface

The question might exist in the minds of men, why hasn't this been written before? World War II has been over since 1945. On second thought, many books have already been written about Hitler's diabolical accomplishments. Why write another?

These thoughts are justifiable, but let me ask you a question: How many of you have heard or read about 'God's keeping power' during those years of unspeakable horror?

With God's help, I'll endeavor to tell you about 'God's keeping power,' as I describe the many times He kept me and saved me from death through His infinite wisdom. I know assuredly that He can and will bring everything to my remembrance about how He revealed Himself to me and the family He has given me. To Him be the glory.

Paula Agauas

Forward

From the first time that the Lord had me testify about His keeping power in my life, someone would always come up to me and tell me how they would love to write it all down for the world to read, but no one ever suggested that I would be the one to write it, and I never thought of it myself.

After 14 years I was asked to speak to a personal evangelism class, which I had done a few times before, pertaining to lessons about the Jewish people. But this time it was different. When I was through, I knew something I had never known before. The only way to minister to others is with love and compassion that can only come from God who is the perfect love.

A few days before the Day of Atonement, I received a telephone call from the Hebrew Christian Fellowship informing us about a prayer meeting that would be held on that day for all the Jews in the world. We were invited to join them, and I said "OK." I told Rubin, my husband, about it, and he said that it would be impossible to attend that day. So I said to him, "Why don't you, Nathan (our son) and I fast and pray that day anyway?

He said, "Fine," and Nathan did too.

Sunday night I saw a girl who was in the class who had heard me. She said, "Why don't you write it down? You should write a book. The way you spoke to the class, you can surely write a book. If you don't, you'll be sinning against God for this testimony cannot be hidden. You're not that dumb, and God will enable you."

I looked at her as if it were not she that was

—

5

speaking, but I heard the sound of my Shepherd's voice. I walked away from her and got Nathan to go home. As we were on our way, I reminded him about the fast the following day.

I awakened in the morning about 7:00 a.m. I sent Nathan off to school, and all of a sudden I had the strong urge to start writing the book. It seemed like I was actually receiving dictation. The only thing I can say is that God's calling is His enabling.

The Word declares that He never leaves Himself without a witness (Acts 14:17). Two weeks before I was through with the writing, I received a postcard from my friend, Bernice, in Florida notifying me of her arrival. For some reason I felt the urgency to finish it before her arrival, and I did.

When we picked her up, she asked me what I had been doing lately. Of course, out of the heart the mouth speaketh (Matthew 12:34). I told her of the writing, and she said, "Why, I knew it all the time. This is just the beginning!"

I asked her what she meant by that. She said, "Just wait and see. About two weeks ago, I received something from the Lord concerning you. I'm not free to tell you yet until it is confirmed, but I can't wait to read what you've written."

I said, "You'll have to read it in order to correct my spelling."

She said, "Of course," and laughed and cried at the same time.

This was on a Saturday about 1:00 p.m. when we picked her up from her nephew's house. I planned on having some other couples over for the evening with the intention of showing some slides from Israel, but the

Paula Agauas

Word declares: *Man plans but God directs* (Proverbs 16:9). So it was that evening.

The telephone rang at 4:00 p.m. It was one of the couples informing me that they'd be unable to come because of a cold. At 5:30 p.m. another telephone call came. It was the other couple telling me that they too couldn't come for some other reason. Then Ruth, the one who had the slides, couldn't start her car. Therefore she couldn't possibly come.

After all that, we awakened to the fact that it must not be God's will for any people to be here, but to have Bernice read this manuscript. I handed her the 173 handwritten pages, and she began reading. As she was reading, she came to the part where she received her confirmation. She said, "As I was dozing, this was strongly impressed on my mind. When Paula writes her book, the title is to be, A Needle in a Haystack."

Paula Agauas

Needle in a Haystack

Introduction

It is Yom Kippur, the Jewish Day of Atonement. My mind goes back to Friday, September 23, 1949, when I arrived in New York from Munich, Germany. I stayed in New York until after the Jewish holidays, when my social worker prepared me for the train journey to Detroit, Michigan.

Because I was unable to speak English, I was pinned with an identification tag. People on the train looked at the tag and began speaking in sign language to me. Fortunately we understood one another. I arrived in Detroit early in the morning and was met by another social worker. She had received my picture so she could recognize me.

I was born on August 20, 1933, and was 16 years old at the beginning of my life in Detroit. I found myself going to school with children in a situation similar to mine. They also didn't know a word of English.

This class was called "The Americanization Class," and the teacher was the most loving person I'd ever met. I had no problem understanding her, because she communicated with a heart full of love.

With this rare ability, she taught the English language to us. It didn't take long before I learned English well enough to be placed in the ninth grade with all the other American children. I began dressing like them and, for the first time, started living as a normal child.

With the Lord's help, I shall explain how all these circumstances came about.

Chapter 1
My Nightmare Begins

I was born in Poland into a Jewish Orthodox home, the youngest of six children. We were four girls and two boys: Frieda, Hannah, Genia, David, Joseph and Paula. (Paula is my name. At times I'm called by my Jewish name of "Pesia".)

My father went to the synagogue on Friday evenings and Saturdays and also said his daily prayers at home. He and his many brothers were excellent tailors, and in this way they earned their living.

Since I, Paula, was the youngest, no doubt I was spoiled. I remember crying a lot if I didn't get my own way. My father did use his belt on me. However, it didn't help for I continued crying into the night. Nevertheless, I loved my father very much. He would have my brother, Joseph, and me sit down with him and repeat after him our daily prayers.

On Saturday afternoons, my father would take us for a walk. Because Saturday was the Sabbath, he always dressed in his best black coat and hat. His long beard added to his striking appearance. We also dressed in our best clothes.

One particular walk took us around a cemetery. Father made this statement which I've never forgotten: "You see these graves? When the Messiah shall come, the trumpet will blow and the dead will come to life again."

Though I was only a little girl – about three years old – my father's words fascinated me. With the faith of a child, it was as if I could actually see this taking place, right then and there!

Needle in a Haystack

We lived in a small village, surrounded by others like it. As one entered the village, the first thing that came into view was a big house, comparable to a co-op. This house belonged to my uncles and to us. My grandparents and great-grandparents lived there too. More people lived in the house in the summertime. Because it was surrounded by beautiful trees and mountains, some of the family from the city came there to rest.

One night I was awakened by everyone in the family yelling, "Fire! Fire! Let's get out!"

Someone had set fire to our chicken coops. Apparently, this wasn't the first of such incidents. Our Polish neighbors wanted us out of there for we were supposed to be the "Christ killers!"

Quite often, when any of our family took a walk, stones were thrown at us by children who claimed we had "killed Jesus." I often asked by father why they did this, but I don't remember his reply.

It must have become too dangerous to live there, for my father moved the family to the city which was named Siedlec. Insofar as I can remember, we had no such problems there.

Thus far, I've told about my father but nothing about my mother. My memory is of my three sisters raising me. I was told that Mother got sick after having her fifth child and was no longer able to take care of her family.

My older brother, Joseph, whom I loved deeply played with me all the time. I remember how good looking he was, for he resembled our mother who was beautiful. I can still see her black hair and light complexion but, most of all, her lovely hands. My oldest

Paula Agauas

sister also looked like Mother.

My other two sisters and brother, David, looked more like Father. We were a close-knit family, and my cousins were like brothers and sisters to us.

One day, while I was alone, I heard sirens. Suddenly a bomb fell on one corner of the house! I was thrown up to the ceiling and back down again! This must have been the first day Germany invaded Poland.

After everything quieted down, the family came home. They had to take refuge in the bomb shelters. When they saw what happened to our house, for reasons of safety, we moved to my aunt's house just outside the city.

When the bombs came down, we had to run to the forest and get under cover. My brother, cousins and I had lots of fun after things quieted down. We liked looking into the deep holes the bombs had made. But this fun didn't last very long, for we eventually moved back to our family home.

After we got back to our house, thankfully we were no longer bothered by our so-called "good neighbors." However, it took no time at all before we were greatly bothered by the German soldiers!

I clearly recall the first incident. Two German soldiers brought my brother, David, home. They pinned him into a corner of the house and began beating him. Finally they left. After that, we were all required to wear bands with a yellow Star of David on our arms so everyone would know we were Jews.

After they tagged us like this, we were ordered to move back to the city. The Germans divided the city by putting barbed wire around one section. Then all the Jews were moved into it.

Needle in a Haystack

We had no house in this section. Consequently we had no choice but to move in with an aunt and her large family. That meant all of us in a one-room apartment. While I can't remember the exact size of the room, the living conditions were not very comfortable with that many people in it.

On one side of the room were three sections of beds, one on top of another. My aunt was in her single bed, and all the rest were on the floor. In the middle of the room was a table. On the other side of the table was the kitchen with a small pot of something cooking on the stove and an area for a few groceries.

Once we Jews were enclosed behind barbed wire in this section of the city – in this 'Ghetto' – the only ones allowed to leave the area were Gentile Poles, young men able to work or for certain other reasons.

One of those *'other reasons'* was when one of my cousins was taken to jail without just cause. My aunt had me take some food to her son while in jail because I looked like a Gentile Pole. My hair was white as snow, and I spoke perfect Polish.

It felt so good walking down there as a Gentile Pole, unafraid of being recognized. I was able to take the food to my cousin without any trouble. He told me to tell his parents that he would be home the following day, but he never got to see that day.

That very night the Germans told all the Jewish young men in his cell that they were being taken in a truck to a concentration camp. As they were being driven the truck stopped, and they were told to get out. Then the machine guns opened fire.

One might ask how I knew all this. I was sent back with more food after my cousin didn't come home, but

Paula Agauas

he wasn't in the jail. So when I asked one of the guards what had happened, he told me the story. I quickly went home and told my family.

After that incident, my aunt seemed to be in bed a lot. She often asked me if I had eaten, and everyone in the room did the same. There was so little food. They gave their food to me, because I was the youngest.

My aunt was dying of hunger. When I went to her bed one morning, she opened her eyes, smiled, and asked me if I had eaten. Then she closed her eyes for the last time. The family had to take her body out for she was dead.

After that my sister Hannah, the second oldest, became very sick with typhoid fever. In her delirium she took a knife and tried to stab me. Everyone in the room grabbed her and tied her to the bed. She accused me of eating up all the food. Thankfully she did recover and had no remembrance whatsoever of the incident.

Because food was so scarce, my father, brothers and two sisters left the house. One by one, they managed to escape from behind the barbed wire. Frieda, my oldest sister, was the only one who was married. She and her husband lived in the infamous Warsaw Ghetto. They and so many others ended up in the gas chambers, or in the fire when, at the end, the Germans set the Warsaw Ghetto up in flames with all the remaining Jews still inside.

After the others escaped, my mother and I were left alone with my cousins. One day when I went out to play, I happened to see an opening in the barbed wire. So I went across. As I did that my mother came out screaming, "Come back! Come back! Come back!"

All of a sudden I saw Germans running and

Needle in a Haystack

shooting. I started to run away. When my mother tried to stop me from running, she was shot dead between the barbed wires. The Gestapo didn't even see me. They saw only my mother when she was screaming for me. Now that I'm a mother myself, I know I'd have done the same thing. Only a mother knows a mother's heart.

Seeing what had happened, I ran into the forest – Poland has many forests – and there I ran into my father and brother, Joseph. I told them what had taken place. They took me to where they were hiding out with other Jews.

A family was there with a little girl who looked like a pretty doll. She cried a lot probably from hunger or any number of things. Fearful that the noise of the crying child might jeopardize the lives of the others, her mother called the Gentile Polish man who was hiding us. She told him to take this little doll of a girl and put her in the barn where she would freeze to death.

"Now where was *that* mother's heart?" one might ask. But who can judge anyone else under such trying circumstances as these? Perhaps the mother knew her daughter was dying anyway. Or possibly the mother should be commended for sacrificing her child for the sake of the others.

Even so, after awhile we all had to split up. The Gentile Polish family was afraid to keep us any longer and told us to leave. We had no choice but to go. They'd have suffered greatly and probably been killed had they been caught hiding us.

Everyone went in different directions. Father told us, "Let the five of us, Joseph, Hannah, Genia, Pesia and I, stay together. We'll go to the village where this widow woman lives alone with her children. I'm sure God has prepared this family to help us. I left some

Paula Agauas

things with her for safe keeping. I'll let her keep them as payment for all I hope she'll do for us."

We went there, and Father was right. She did take us in. Also living with her was a Russian soldier that had parachuted into Poland. He was hiding from the Germans, but the villagers let him alone for he was a great help to the widow woman. He too became a help to us in many ways.

When the widow became fearful of keeping us, for her life was greatly endangered, the Russian was the one who comforted her. He also made sure she cooked enough food for all of us, and then he'd bring it to us in the barn where we were hiding. Sometimes he was the look-out man so we could go into the house and eat. This was a real treat for us.

Chapter 2
A Hiding Place

You are my hiding place

You always pick me up

Whenever I am alone

I will trust in you

One day, while we were in the house, somehow the villagers found out we were there. They came after us with destructive weapons, like clubs and potato choppers that were used to chop potatoes for the pigs. These same villagers were at one time supposedly my father's best friends. Yet they turned on us as quickly and as easily as if they'd been our lifelong enemies.

Among the things Father had left with the widow was his sewing machine. Before the villagers had a chance to get into the house, Father said to us, "Quickly, hide behind the large stove!" Then the widow's children got on the bed and started jumping up and down and singing. My father sat behind his sewing machine and began to sew. In order to save us, he was trying to make it look as if he was the only one there.

The villagers came in full force, demanding to know where my father's children were. The brave children jumping on the bed told them we weren't there. The villagers grabbed my father and savagely started beating him with the clubs and chopping him with the potato choppers! When I saw this, I opened my mouth to scream, but my brother and sisters held my mouth so I couldn't let out a sound.

Father moaned in agony, but somehow he prevented himself from crying out. Finally they stopped

Paula Agauas

beating him, gave him up for dead and left. But I refused to believe he wasn't alive. I tried hard to listen, hoping I could still hear him breathing.

At last we were able to come out from behind the stove and rushed over to Father. He was full of holes and bleeding all over, but thank God he was still alive! The widow woman helped us all out of the house to the barn where we managed to put Father on the hay. Then she got some iodine and tended to Father's wounds.

However, after she took care of him she said, "When you are well enough, I want you to take Joseph and Pesia out of here. As you can see, it's not safe for all of you to stay in one place. But I'll help your two daughters, Hannah and Genia, to make out some working papers for Germany. I'm sure they'll be able to pass as Gentile Polish girls, for they're light complexioned. The German government is taking Polish girls to Germany to work in different places of employment."

When my father was well enough to walk, he took my brother, Joseph, and me away from the widow woman's house. The three of us moved only by night and hid in barn lofts. These lofts were so dark and frightening that I wished myself to be a cow, or a horse, or a bird, anything except a human being. I felt if I were an animal I would be able to see the daylight and not be afraid.

As soon as it became dark enough so we couldn't be seen, we moved from place to place. Oh, how I longed to lie down on a nice, soft bed and go to sleep. Now the only bed I knew was hay, which was at least warm.

One day as we were hiding in a barn, Father was

Needle in a Haystack

praying on one side of the barn. I became very tired and wanted so badly to go to sleep but couldn't see a place where I might lie down. It was during the winter months and terribly cold. I happened to look across to the opposite side from where my father was praying.

There it was – my warm bed of hay! I ran to it and, without telling Father where I was, dug myself into the hay and immediately fell asleep.

I remember my brother Joseph, out of breath, waking me up. "I just came back to see if you were alive. Father had said to me that it was no use. You were dead, but I refused to listen to him and had to see for myself.

"You see, the Germans somehow spotted us and started shooting and beating on the door. We had no time to wake you but had to run. After we were a distance away, I decided to come after you. Come, let's go to Father. I'm sure when he sees you, he'll look at you as if you are a ghost!"

After what Joseph said, I knew I had to get out of there quickly and be reunited with Father. When we got there, Joseph said to him, "See, Father, I was right. She *is* alive!"

Father was the one who looked like a ghost. He was very pale as he hugged me and cried, "Thank God you're alive!"

I was very hungry and asked him if I could have something to eat. He answered, "Let's go to our old neighbors. Surely they'll give us some food."

These neighbors that my father had grown up with told us to go into the barn. They would bring us some hot food. But instead of food, these so-called 'good

18

neighbors' brought clubs and other weapons with the intention of killing us!

When Father spotted them, he told us to run after him. We ran and ran. Being so little, I was the last one, but they didn't catch up to us. When we stopped running, we forgot about the hunger and found a place to sleep in some other deserted barn.

We had to move on in order to try to find some food. My trusting father said, "I know a family that will help us. They need me to do some sewing for the family. Let's go there." So that's where we went. They did accept us, giving us some hot food to eat, and Father did some sewing for them.

We were there for a week when a group of Father's 'friends' came in and took my father and brother away. I was just sitting there with everyone else in the room, not saying a word. However, just as soon as my father and brother were taken out, I had a strong feeling I should get out of there quickly! I ran into the barn right by the house and dug myself into the hay.

Just as soon as I did this, the people of the house became hostile and started screaming, "Where is she? We have to get her over there with her father and brother. Let them all be killed together!"

This was the first time I remember feeling truly scared, thinking, "What am I going to do without my father and brother? Where can I go alone?" I escaped such further frightening thoughts by falling asleep.

I was awakened by someone calling my name. The voice sounded like Joseph's. Miraculously, it was indeed Joseph. Bleeding all over but still alive, he said to me, "We must leave at once. We can't stay here."

Needle in a Haystack

"But we must wait for Father," I insisted.

Joseph hung his head sadly as he said, "Father is dead."

"No, no," I argued. "You are here, and I thought you too were dead. So let's wait awhile. Maybe Father will come for us."

Joseph, exhausted and bleeding from his severe wounds, was almost glad to stop for a rest. We waited and waited.

Suddenly we heard something. It was Father! To me he looked like the skeleton of a dead man come to life again. Perhaps the trumpet had blown, and he was raised from the dead to come back and take us away to safety. In these horrible times, could not such wonders also happen?

The three of us walked away from there into the bitter cold. The snow was so deep in the fields that it came past my knees. Once again I was getting tired and sleepy, and the snow felt nice and soft and warm. I said to Joseph, "I'm going to lie down in the snow and go to sleep."

Joseph cried out, "No! Come on. You'll die if you fall asleep!" And he dragged me out of the snow.

I could hear Father ahead of us shouting at Joseph, "Let her stay! Let her stay!"

But Joseph refused to leave me. "No! She's coming with us." As he pulled me out of the snow, tears were streaming down his face.

When we got to a safe place – I don't remember where – it wasn't so cold anymore, even though there were large patches of snow on the ground here and

20

Paula Agauas

there. This must have been near to spring in 1943.

Father had cut off his beard so he would look less conspicuously like a Jew. Nevertheless, in spite of near starvation, he still refused to eat anything out of the pots of Gentiles. It was against the Jewish religion. He lived on bread and water, and fruit when we could find any. However, he told me to eat *everything*, even pork, and that it wouldn't be sinful for us since we were only children.

One day Father heard that in one village a family was hiding a Jew, and the Germans found out about it. The German government had posters hanging all over Poland ordering the people not to hide Jews. If they were found hiding even one Jew, all of the villagers would be taken to concentration camps. The children would be taken away from their parents, and the entire village would be burned to the ground.

This is exactly what happened to one of the villages, and Father somehow heard about it. He also heard that as the children were being transported somewhere by train, some of them managed to escape.

When Poland was alerted about it, the Polish government issued a statement saying: "If any children show up in the villages, families are to take them in and keep them until after the war. Maybe some of the parents will live through the war and reclaim their children."

It was becoming impossible for us to go on. Father called Joseph and me to tell us of the situation we were in. He said to me, "Pesia, you look like a Polish Gentile. Your hair is white as snow, and you speak like any Polish girl. All over Poland it's known about the escaped children. You're going to have a Polish name. Your

Needle in a Haystack

name will no longer be 'Pesia Atramentowicz'. Your name will now be 'Paula Siurek'.

"You'll tell them you had one brother, Joseph, and no sisters or other brothers. That way you won't have to remember any new names, which would have to be Polish. Most of all, **pray to Jesus**, and they'll believe you're a Polish Gentile. After the war, go to the United States – to Detroit – and your aunt will take you in."

I can remember my brother, Joseph, crying and saying, "No, Father! She can't be left alone. I'll take care of her."

I cried, telling Father I wanted to die with them and not alone, but Father said nothing after that.

Chapter 3
Guardian Angel

One morning I awakened to find myself all alone, but then a strange thing happened. From as far back as I can remember, I had always had a fear of being left alone. Yet that morning I was not alone. There was a *'Presence'* with me, one that is difficult to explain. I called it my *'Guardian Angel.'* I had no fear whatsoever. I was surrounded by an invisible army.

Then I remembered Father also saying, "Maybe your sisters will be able to help you."

Therefore I thought, *I'll go to the place where they're hiding.* But I didn't know east from west. I needn't have worried. My invisible *'Guide'* showed me the way.

When I knocked at the door, the widow woman opened it and greeted me. I asked her to have my sisters come out, but she said they weren't there. I knew better, for my invisible *'Guide'* told me differently. I said to the widow woman, "I know they're here." Finally, my sister Hannah came out.

I told Hannah that Father had left me. He had told me what I was to do, and perhaps they could help me. My other sister never came out, but I knew she was there.

After Hannah cleaned me up from all the lice I had collected on the way, she told me to do as Father had instructed me. Then she told me to leave. I left, but I said to myself, "I never want to see my sisters again!"

They were afraid of me. If the Germans captured me and tortured me to find out where they were, I

Needle in a Haystack

might have given them away. If I didn't know where they were, at least they were safer. Again, no one knows what war can do to a person.

Father did say that I was to walk as far as I could to where people didn't know us. So I left my sisters and began walking. As I walked, a couple in a horse and buggy drove by me. They stopped and I heard the woman say, "Isn't this girl the daughter of Atramentowicz?" But I continued walking.

Hunger was overcoming me, so I decided to stop when I reached the next village. When I reached the village, I knocked at the door of a house. A woman answered the door, and I said, "I'm a Jewish girl. My father left me, and I'm all alone. Will you please give me a piece of bread?"

The woman told me to wait, that she'd be right back. But the *'Voice'* told me to run. So I ran! I ran to a haystack, got on top and dug myself into it. No sooner had I managed to do this than the woman brought the Germans with her. The Germans demanded, "Well, where is she?"

The woman answered, "She couldn't have disappeared into thin air!"

Then I heard the Germans say, "We'll push our bayonets into the haystack and see if she's hiding in there."

I thought, *This is the end of me!* The bayonets kept coming closer and closer. One of them was coming straight at my heart and was just a hair away, when I heard one of them say, "She's not here, you stupid woman." And the bayonet was pulled out!

I lay there for awhile trying to catch my breath.

Paula Agauas

Then I decided to dig myself out of the haystack. I stuck my head out. Lo and behold, it had become so foggy that I couldn't see in any direction. I clearly remembered that when I crawled up in the haystack the sky was clear and the sun was out. But not now.

This turn of the weather made me unafraid to move out of there, for I would be under cover of the fog. Not knowing which way to go, I followed my *'Guide's'* direction and walked on.

Finally, I was nearing another village. This time I thought that I'd better remember what my father had told me to say. As I approached the village, I saw children playing with snowballs. I hadn't played with other kids in such a long time. I decided to run up there.

However, before I had a chance to take one step, *something* physically pushed me to the left which was the first house in the village. I had no choice but to obey.

I walked into the yard, knocked at the door and a woman answered. Having learned my lesson well from the haystack incident, I remembered to say everything the way my father had told me.

There was much explaining I didn't have to do, for she had heard about some of the children running away from the train. She told me to come in and called her husband and two of her sons who were at home.

I found out they also had two other sons who were living away from home. The two living at home were farmers, while the third was an accountant – a widower with a daughter living in Warsaw – and the fourth was a veterinarian who was married and had a little boy. The woman and her husband had no daughters. They were

Needle in a Haystack

the wealthiest people in that town, and all the villagers worked for them.

After the woman introduced me to her two sons, the older son said, "We'd better take her over to the sheriff's office and register her."

Off we went with the villagers following us there. It seems that in a small village everyone knows what is going on everywhere else.

The whole village wanted to keep me! The sheriff's wife had never been able to have children. So the sheriff and his wife wanted to keep me for their own. Nevertheless, I was wishing someone would ask me where I wanted to go.

Immediately the sheriff said, "Let's ask the girl where she'd like to go."

I already knew where I was to go and said, "The first house to the left." Who can say that God doesn't prepare a table in the presence of the enemy (Psalm 23:5)?

Paula Agauas

Chapter 4
New Grandparents

The couple was old enough to be my grandparents. Perhaps that's why, on the way from the sheriff's office, they told me to call them 'Grandma' and 'Grandpa.'

When we arrived home, Grandma said, "This child must be hungry." So she cooked some soup and gave it to me. I took one spoon of it, and as soon as I swallowed it my stomach began to hurt. I literally crawled on the floor, because the pain was so bad.

Grandma couldn't have known that my insides had shrunk from my not having eaten in such a long time. When she realized the situation, she massaged my stomach and gave me only tiny bits at a time. Grandma did this for quite a few weeks until she brought me back to normal again.

Then they enrolled me in school and catechism. I was already ten years of age, and this was my very first time in school. The school wasn't in this village, but now that I was stronger I was able to walk with the other children to the village where the school was.

After school I had chores to do, such as milk the cows, feed the chickens and gather the eggs. Since some of my duties included watching over the cows and other animals, I became a real cowgirl. I could even ride a horse bareback to round up the cattle.

At harvest time, I had to be an example for the other workers, meaning I had to be the fastest. I was proud to be such an example.

I loved the open spaces, the fresh air, the green grass, the flowers and everything growing in the fields.

Needle in a Haystack

It was as if I'd been some kind of animal that had been locked up for years in a cage, ready for slaughter, but someone had mercy on it and set it free.

After we had finished the catechism studies, the priest brought a basket filled with scrolls of saints. The priest said, "Now close your eyes and put your hands in the basket. Whatever picture you take will be your patron saint."

Then I remembered that Father had said to me, "Pray to Jesus, and they'll believe you're Catholic."

I thought, *If I pick the picture of Jesus, then I can pray to Him like Father said. But if I pick a saint, then I'll have to pray to that saint instead.* God must have heard my thoughts for He granted my heart's desire.

When I put my hand in the basket and picked the picture, it was the picture of Jesus with the Bleeding Heart! As I looked at it, these words were impressed in my mind. "Don't be afraid. I've gone through the same thing you're going through. I am a Jew! I've overcome the world, and so will you." Yet it seemed as if the only thing I heard was the part about, "I am a Jew."

As far as I was concerned, there were no more Jews in the world. I was the only Jew left alive! Often I was full of fear because of this thought, but now I had another Jew – someone to talk to and not just to pray to.

It's impossible for me to describe what kind of joy came into my being through this wonderful knowledge. I remember wanting to go to church more often, as if the church were my home. I loved to take Communion. As I partook of the wafers, He was so much alive and not dead. I never questioned His being alive. To me He was the other Jew. He filled me with such love for Him

Paula Agauas

that I felt I was being nurtured in an abundance of love.

By now you're acquainted with my using various phrases such as, *'Guide,' 'Voice'* and *'Invisible Presence.'* When I looked at the picture, I heard the very same Voice of my Guide and my Guardian Angel, and I felt the same loving Presence. And yet He was a Jew like me.

Living with a family again and having a roof over my head was a new experience, especially the great change from a strict Orthodox Jewish home to a Roman Catholic home. However, it didn't take me long to adjust after what I'd been through. No more hiding from place to place trying to escape the hunters. Not only did we have to hide from the Germans but from the Gentile Poles as well.

The Polish hunters received five pounds of sugar for every Jew they turned in. Compared to these vicious human beings, ferocious wild animals would have been welcomed.

One evening as we all sat at dinner, the sons told me what they thought was an exciting story. They were laughing hilariously about it. "Just before you came here, Paula, a Jew came to our village for protection. We gave him protection all right! We tied him to a haystack when the weather was freezing and left him there overnight. Can you guess what happened to him?" They laughed and laughed, and I laughed with them. They all loved me.

Once again I had a family, and they were glad there was a girl in the house. I liked the three older sons, but I certainly didn't care for the younger one. He must have been around sixteen or seventeen.

When we sat down to eat at the table, each of us

had our own silverware, but we didn't have individual plates. Grandma would put one giant bowl with potatoes, pork and gravy in the middle of the table. Then everyone would dig in.

I'd always get sick to my stomach, not because of the food or because we all ate from the same bowl. It was because Stefan had a runny nose. I'd scream, "Grandma, have Stefan wipe his nose!" But no sooner had he done it, then it started running again.

I was losing weight and getting sicker by the day, but they couldn't understand why. Finally, they took me to a doctor. He told Grandma to put me on a special diet. After that my sickness left me, for I had my own plate.

The Christmas season was very exciting. We didn't have store-bought ornaments such as we have here. We had to make our own. All of us girls would get together in each other's homes to make all kinds of decorations for our Christmas trees. We also made cookies, cutting them into different shapes and sizes, and hung them on the trees. During our festive preparations, we sang beautiful Christmas carols.

When Christmas Eve arrived, all of us went to the church to look at the Baby Jesus. Eventually I discovered it was only a doll, but at first I believed the doll was actually real. It was wonderful to come home from church and eat at midnight.

In the morning, we rode in sleds as the music of the bells attached to the horses rang out. It was all breathtaking for me, and I loved to be in church. At that time I was not a Jew. Even the thought of being a Jew was completely gone from my mind.

One morning when I awakened, Grandma said to

Paula Agauas

me, "Paula, last night you must have had a nightmare. You screamed and talked in a language that was hard for me to understand."

Somehow I had the presence of mind to say to her, "You know when someone talks in his sleep, it's really impossible to understand him."

She responded with some relief, "So that's why I couldn't understand what you were saying."

Nonetheless, I knew full well the language in which I had spoken must have been Jewish. After that I was afraid to go to sleep for fear I might have another nightmare like that one, and the next time she'd find me out. I didn't know what to do.

As I lay awake – trying very hard not to fall asleep – I remembered at last what my father had told me. "Pray to Jesus, and they'll believe you're Catholic."

Therefore, I prayed, "Please, Jesus, make me forget this night the Jewish language, so that when I awake in the morning I'll not even remember how to say 'no' or 'yes' in Jewish. Please Jesus, for Father told me to pray to you."

I fell asleep immediately. After many nights of not being able to sleep, I slept peacefully. Even so, I still dreamed a lot, for I seemed to relive everything when I slept.

When I awakened the following morning, I was fully aware of the request I had made to Jesus before I had trusted myself to go to sleep. I tried to recall how to say 'yes' and 'no' in Jewish, but I was unable to do so! I could have jumped to the ceiling from the bed out of pure joy. I screamed, "Jesus! Jesus! You did it! You did it!"

Grandma rushed into the room. She had absolutely

no inkling of what was going on. She asked me, "What's happening?"

How glad I was to tell her. "I'm happy because last night I prayed to Jesus that I'd have no more nightmares, and I didn't! And I had the best night's sleep since I came here." Grandma was happy with me.

The winter months were exciting, especially in the evening for the evenings were long. Before it became dark, I would clean out the kerosene lamps which we had to use because the villages had no electricity.

The ladies and their daughters would get together in each other's homes with their spinning wheels and spin out the yarn and then weave the yarn into material. They taught me how to do this, and I was getting very good at it. Another thing we'd do was to chop cabbage and put it into barrels to make sauerkraut.

When daylight came, Grandma would bring in some fresh water for the villages had no running water either. Then the boys and Grandma and I would milk the cows. Grandpa was the lazy type. He was always cold, so he sat by the wood burning stove. Since this was the only heating unit in the entire house, it burned all night and day. It was also where the cooking was done.

After the cows were milked, we had to feed them as well as the pigs, sheep, goats, rabbits, horses and chickens. Only after the animals were fed did the rest of us sit down to eat.

Our breakfast in the village was a heavy farmer's breakfast, consisting of things we eat for supper in this country. After breakfast I went off to school with a group of other children. All of us trudged through the deep snow.

Paula Agauas

Chapter 5
Fortune Telling Resistance

I had a girlfriend whose name was Angie. She was especially nice to me, and we ate together at lunchtime. Angie was a little older than I and very protective of me. She was the child of a poor unwed mother who could hardly make ends meet.

Since I lived with a family that hired the villagers in that town to work in their fields, I was able to help Angie and her mother get a job working. They were paid with everything that grew in the fields.

Angie's mother had a hobby of telling people's fortunes through cards. Some of the things she told were quite memorable. For instance, one day three men of the village came to her to have their fortunes told.

She looked at the cards and told the men, "Tomorrow morning the three of you will be dead!" They walked out laughing loudly at her. I happened to be there that day and sure enough in the morning all three men lay dead – just as she had said. I was so used to seeing dead people that I thought nothing of it, particularly after witnessing the following incident which has never left my mind.

Two Russians had parachuted into our village and were found by the German soldiers. The Germans forced the Russians to dig their own graves deep enough for them to stand in. They were told to jump in the graves and cover themselves to their armpits with the same dirt. Then the Germans shot the Russians in the head and threw the rest of the dirt over them.

The German soldiers placed on top of the graves a

Needle in a Haystack

marker made out of the dead men's scarves which they had taken from the necks of the Russians. They took two sticks, stuck them in the graves and then hung a bloody scarf on each of the sticks. The other children and I quietly watched as all this took place. I could just see myself being in that grave.

Now I must tell you why the three men were shot that morning. About two weeks before this happened, during some nights while the villagers were in deep sleep, the 'underground movement' came into the homes and helped themselves to food, clothing and anything else they needed. One morning I discovered my very best Sunday shoes and dress had been taken from the attic.

One of those nights, I was awakened by a flashlight shining in my face. I opened my eyes to see the face of my cousin! I started to say something to him, but he put his hand on my mouth and said, "Don't say a word right now. I'll see you tomorrow. Look for me. I'll be in disguise. I'll probably come when you're out in the pasture with the animals. I'll tell the others not to take anything else from this house, nor will we ever come here again for food." My cousin was true to his word. Our home was never ransacked again.

I was so excited about seeing him, I couldn't go back to sleep. I waited impatiently for daylight to come, so I could ride out to the fields where the green pastures were.

On that day they were greener than ever. At that time I was a real cowgirl, riding those horses without a saddle, but you couldn't get me on a horse now even *with* a saddle.

I looked anxiously down the road to see if anyone

Paula Agauas

was coming. The hours seemed longer than ever, but I could tell time to the minute by the way my shadow went with the sun.

Finally he came. What a reunion! He asked me about everything, and I told him all I could. Then he asked me, "How do you like it here? If they don't treat you right, you can come with us and you'll be safe. We have all kinds including Poles and Russians that have parachuted in. We're fighting this war, and there are quite a few from this town that are working with us."

I asked him who they were, but he wouldn't tell me. I told him I'd like to remain where I was because the people were treating me very well. He said, "Shalom," and left.

After that I didn't see him again until the day the three men were shot. He came to see me in the late afternoon and asked me if I had seen or heard about three other men being shot.

I answered, "Yes, I saw those three men lying dead on the street this morning when we were on our way to school."

Then he told me, "Those three men were part of us. We trusted each other, but they heard me say you were my cousin. I told them where you were staying so I could instruct them not to go there for anything.

"They were found out just in time, for they were going to give you up to the Germans. Therefore, we had to take care of them that morning!"

Only then did I realize that those three men lying dead in the road were the three men whose cards Angie's mother had read, telling them they would be dead the following day. What keeping power of God!

Needle in a Haystack

Although I couldn't have known it at *that* time, I certainly know *now* that it was the Lord my God who had watched over me and kept me through every danger and crisis those many years.

The winter was soon over, and I looked forward to Easter. I loved helping prepare the baskets, color the eggs and neatly put them in the baskets. When Good Friday came, the priest came to the village, and everyone came out with their baskets to be sprinkled with holy water.

On Easter Sunday morning we all went to church. I couldn't think of anyone being as devout a Catholic as I. I can't remember how long after we were confirmed that the other children and I went to church to be anointed with oil and given a saintly name by the priest. Since I loved the name of Saint Teresa, the priest named me 'Teresa.'

My Jewishness had left me to such a degree that I found myself thinking, *Why, I'm not really a true Catholic, for I'm not baptized!* This really bothered me.

One day I decided that I had to confess this to the priest at my next confession. *He'll keep it a secret and secretly baptize me. Then I'll be a perfect Catholic*, I thought.

Finally, one Sunday morning I said to Angie, "Let's go to confession." Angie agreed, so off we went. Little did she know my true intention.

We arrived at church early enough for confession. I saw the priest sitting in his booth listening to another confessor, and I waited patiently for my turn. As I approached the window of the booth and was just about to begin talking, something made me look toward the main entrance. Lo and behold! I saw there one of the

36

Paula Agauas

girlfriends with whom I used to play at home.

When I recognized her, the fear of her identifying me gripped my heart and caused me to faint. I was awakened by Angie telling me that I had fainted just before confession. When she asked me what happened, I answered weakly, "I truly don't know. We'd better go home." And we did.

That same Sunday Grandma went to mass. When she came home, she told us what the priest's main message had been. It went like this: "God was taking vengeance on the Jews for they had killed Jesus, and therefore, it was God's will that the Jews should be killed."

How do you like that? No one can *ever* tell me that the true and living Jesus – the Jew – was not with me! He isn't dead but alive! At that time I never questioned why they said He had been killed by the Jews. Yet He had identified Himself to me as One who is alive and not dead. I was positive of that, and no one could have been as happy as I was to know that I wouldn't be the only Jew left alive in this world. There was another, and He was Jesus Christ, *the Jew!*

After that incident, I never again wanted to be baptized. As far as I was concerned, I was a better Catholic than the ones who were sprinkled at infancy. I knew a *personal* God of love and protection. I couldn't go to that priest for protection. Even though he was called 'Father' by everyone, he wasn't *my* Father. I had a better Father, a Father whom I could trust. One who would never reveal my secrets to the enemy.

The church we attended was situated not too far from the villages where my original family was well known, and often the people who came to this church were known to me. After I became aware of this fact, I had no desire to go to that church again, even though it was the most beautiful one in the area and closest to me.

My present family, Grandma, Grandpa and the others, couldn't understand why I had become so set against going to this church. It was much closer to home than the church I now chose to go to. I told them, "It's much more fun walking to the other one. Besides, I like the priest better, for he is much nicer."

Of course, Angie said the same thing, and she would be the first one of all the other boys and girls to agree with me. Before long most of the children began going to the church I had chosen over the one closest to home.

Little did I know that Angie and her mother knew about my being a Jew, for they never let on. They were working with the underground movement, *'The Resistance.'* This was told to me *after* the war through a letter I received in Germany from Angie. She also sent me my Communion dress, but I don't remember what I did with it. In addition, she sent the picture of my first Communion taken with two other girls, which I still have.

One afternoon on the way from school, a woman passed by me. I recognized her and tried to hide my face, but she noticed me and said something to one of the kids. Then she left. I didn't think much of it at the time, but a week later she happened to show up at the house. She was invited in by Grandma and given something to eat. Then she asked my name and Grandma told her about me.

Paula Agauas

Paula (1st from left) holding the picture of 'Jesus – the other Jew' that, with eyes closed, she had randomly selected from the basket filled with scrolls of saints. He was now her patron saint.

The woman said, "I come from Shmiary. A family lived there by the name of Atramentowicz, and they had a younger daughter whose name was Pesia." Turning to me she said, "I tell you, Paula, you look just like her. When I saw you walking from school, I recognized you. Thinking you were her, I asked one of the girls where

39

you lived."

I laughed and said, "It's possible she resembled me, but how many cows have you seen that look alike? And though they have the same spots, could you tell them apart?"

She laughed too and said, "That's true." Then she excused herself and left the house.

Grandma remarked, "What a nerve to come here thinking such a thing."

Laughingly I asked her, "What would you do if that were true?"

She replied, "I'd do nothing, but the boys would do to you what they did to the Jew. They would tie you to the haystack to be frozen to death or get five pounds of sugar as a reward for turning you over to the Germans."

It didn't take long after this incident until some of the children started calling me 'Jew.' It finally came to the point where Grandma called me in and said, "I think you'll have to be sent away for a little while to live with my son, the veterinarian, and his family until this quiets down. It's not right that you should go through such unfair persecution. After it has quieted down, you'll come back."

I was very happy at this suggestion, for the church I liked was right around the corner from her son's home.

After awhile, I did come back home and all was well. My friends were very happy to see me and called me no more names. Everything seemed to be going all right, or so I thought.

Grandma told me that her older son – the accountant from Warsaw – was arriving with a friend of

Paula Agauas

his for the weekend, and we'd better clean up the house.

When they arrived, we all had dinner together. The friend was left alone with me and began to ask me all kinds of questions. After the questioning was over he called the family together saying, "She isn't Jewish. I can swear it."

Of course, they were relieved. But little did they know how relieved I was! After that we were one happy family. So happy, in fact, that Grandma told me that Stefan, her youngest son, was going to marry me when I was old enough.

That was all I had to hear – a lifetime with that snotty-nose boy with both of us eating from the same dish! To me this was worse than being found out.

I remember always kneeling down by my bed before going to sleep and talking to my Jesus, the other Jew. That night I really poured out my heart. I cried and cried. I remember not wanting to live after that. Nevertheless, I got up from my knees and went to sleep peacefully.

I awoke the next morning hardly thinking of what Grandma had said to me. I even began liking Stefan with his runny nose, and things got on very well. Then Stefan was drafted into the army. He wrote letters to the family, and I was the one who answered them.

The other son was always busy in the fields, but I liked him. He took very good care of me, just like an older brother would. Then he got married. I didn't like him as well, because he seemed to like his wife better than he did me. His actions were beyond my understanding.

One day some of the neighbors got together and came to the house. They demanded that I be taken to

Needle in a Haystack

the fortune teller. When Grandma wanted to know why, they told her, "There's a rumor going around that she's Jewish. We've come to take her to the fortune teller who will tell us for *sure*. Her cards will tell the truth! Remember the three men? How they were killed after the cards showed they would be shot, just as she said? Everything she said so far came true."

Grandma gave in saying, "Very well, we'll do as you say, and you'll hear for yourselves that all of this is only gossip."

Off we went to the fortune teller, Angie's mother. When we arrived, she seemed to be prepared for us and already had the cards on the table. This time I was scared. I knew that everything she said came to pass, and for sure she'd see in the cards that I was Jewish.

After we sat down, she proceeded to look at the cards and said, "I see this girl as not being too long with us. She is being taken to a faraway country where she'll be safe. And the country she'll live in will be very good to her. She is not Jewish, as you have been suspecting, for I don't see it in the cards."

I could hardly contain myself upon hearing her statement. Grandma said with great satisfaction, "I hope you'll leave us alone now that you know the truth." Then we all left and went home.

On the way, I became very tired. I told Grandma I'd like to leave home for a little while and stay with her son – the one who lived not very far from my church. At the same time, I'd have a good rest from the people who had put me through all this testing. Grandma agreed and personally took me to her son's house.

The couple had a little boy who was a real monster! I mean he was really spoiled. One Sunday morning he

42

Paula Agauas

was helping me peel potatoes. For some reason he became very angry with me and took his knife and purposely cut my hand. He made a deep cut, from which I still have a scar. Had I been able to see a doctor, I'm sure I would've needed quite a few stitches. But when I looked at the cut, the blood was there. Yet I was *not* bleeding.

It was a fascinating sight. They bandaged it up, and in about two days there was not a sign of an open cut except for the scar. I called *that* a miracle! No infection had a chance to set in, and I became very conscious of the fact that *God* was my doctor.

I stayed quite often with the veterinarian son and his family during the year of 1944 and through February or March of 1945. At that time the Russians occupied Poland, and the Poles were happy to be freed from the hand of Adolph Hitler. They thought that Russia would be their deliverer, but instead the Russians came in like "an angel of light" (2 Corinthians 11:14), making many false promises.

Some of the poor Poles were very happy with the promises, for they were told that there'd be no more rich families. Everybody would be equal. All the lands would be divided up equally, and everyone would be working in their own fields.

The Russians kept their promise and divided up the lands, including most of the land that belonged to Grandma and Grandpa. This was very hard on them. It didn't take long before the Poles found out that the Russian way of equality was not such a good idea after all. They learned that even though they had equal shares and were supposed to work in their own fields, they didn't really work for themselves. Instead, they became slaves to the Russians!

Needle in a Haystack

Chapter 6
Kidnapped

When the war was over, I felt I really had nothing to fear. *The Germans are gone,* I thought to myself, *so why should I fear?* Yet, I still had this fear of the Poles and with good reason. After all, were they not the ones who had been after our lives as well as the Germans?

One day I was called into the house by Grandma's daughter-in-law, the wife of the veterinarian. She informed me that Grandma had arrived with a Russian to take me home. Every nerve in my body was alerted as I entered the room.

I saw Grandma, and then I had to look way up to see the man for he was quite tall. You can imagine my surprise when I saw the face of the parachuted Russian who had hidden in the widow woman's house where my sisters had stayed.

Naturally, I was very happy to see him, but I dared not show my feelings. Quickly the thought came to me, *Maybe he feels differently now, or maybe he has become like my father's 'friends.' I won't let on that I know him.*

Grandma said, "This young man claims he knows you. He says you're Paula Atramentowicz." He looked at me excitedly while Grandma was talking.

When she was through, he came over to hug me, but I backed away and said, "Grandma, I don't know who this man is. Whatever he's told you is a lie!"

Grandma said, "I told him that he's wasting his time by coming here."

The Russian said, "I've brought your sister,

44

Hannah, with me. She's waiting for you at the house. We've come to take you away from here."

Grandma agreed, "It's true. There's a woman waiting for you. She claims you're her sister."

The Russian continued to coax me. "You don't have to be afraid anymore. The war is over. The Germans are gone."

In my childlike mind, I thought, *But the Poles are still here.*

Grandma, wanting to get the matter settled and over with, urged me, "The best thing for you to do is come with us and meet this lady who claims to be your sister. Let her see she's made a mistake. On second thought, you don't have any sisters but only one brother."

At last, Grandma said the correct thing. I looked at her, and then it was I who firmly insisted, "You're right. Let's go."

The three of us got on the sled buggy that the horses pulled, and the Russian held the reins. On the way home, he began telling me what had happened to my father and my brother, even though I tried to stop him by repeating to him, "I'm *not* that girl!"

He paid no attention to what I said but continued his story. "After he left you, your father stopped by every so often with your brother, Joseph. Then finally he had to leave Joseph also but not for long.

"Afterwards, Joseph was killed in a village nearby – not by the Germans, but by the *'good neighbors.'* Three months before the Russians occupied Poland, the same *'good neighbors'* killed your father. I think they buried them both in the same place, but I'm not sure."

Needle in a Haystack

I remember trying to hold my tears in and kept my face down. It was a miracle that I didn't let my emotions be known to them. Only the living God could have kept me in that frame of mind.

The Russian went on, "Your sisters, Hannah and Genia, lived through the war by being sent to Germany as Gentile Poles. Somehow, they managed to escape to Switzerland. After the war they decided to return to find out if anyone was left alive." Before he was able to pass on any more information, we were home.

I entered the room, and there was indeed a neatly dressed lady sitting in a chair. Grandma introduced me to her, but I didn't recognize her as being my sister, Hannah. The lady began telling me how she found out where I was.

She said, "When Genia and I arrived from Switzerland, we really didn't know what to do or what procedures to take in finding survivors. Someone finally told us to go to the city where we came from. They said we'd probably find the place where the returning Jews were registering, and that's how families were being reunited. We went to the registry and asked if anyone else by this name had registered there."

The lady continued her story. "The registrar told us, 'Your cousin registered himself and also a little girl whose name was Paula. Your cousin instructed us as follows: If anything happens to me before I'm able to get her out of there, make sure that someone else gets her out.'

"A few days later," said the lady, "we found out at the registry, someone claimed that our cousin entered a store and made this remark. '*Now* we're going to avenge ourselves for the killing of our families!'"

46

Paula Agauas

Taking a deep breath, the lady went on. "Then the registrar told us, 'As he was leaving the store, someone shot him in the back. We were just getting ready to send a man to the village to get the little girl, for he had told us the name of the village was Trzczyniec. But now that you're here, you know where to go and can get her out of there.' And now you know, Paula, how we managed to find you."

Of course, I had to listen to her talk, but I still didn't know her. As far as I was concerned, she was a perfect stranger. I told her, "But you're not my sister. I have no sisters."

Grandma then asked her, "Do you know her?"

She answered, "Yes, she's my sister."

But I insisted, "She's not telling the truth."

This caused the lady to proceed naming all my family and where we had lived. She included, like the Russian, that my father and my brother had been killed by my father's best friends just three months before the war was over. She said I should go with them for my life would never be safe there because I was Jewish, and so on.

I still couldn't recognize her and thought, *They're really doing a great job trying to deceive me.*

Finally, the woman gave up and said to the Russian, "There's no use. She cannot recognize me. In fact, she doesn't know me. We'll have to leave her here."

As they were opening the door, I recognized her voice. I called her back by name, "Hannah, Hannah, come back!"

Grandma stood there in shock, saying, "Paula, you don't know what you're saying. You aren't Jewish."

Needle in a Haystack

I was relieved to tell her, "Yes, I'm Jewish. She's my sister. I recognized her voice as she was leaving, but it doesn't mean I'm going with her. I don't want to be a Jew anymore. I want to be Catholic. The Jewish people have to suffer too much. So I'm through being a Jew. I want to be baptized, that is, *if* you still want me. Then I'll be a real Catholic."

Grandma grabbed me and hugged me and assured me, "Of course I still want you! We'll talk to the priest, and he'll be glad to baptize you."

My sister had no choice but to leave me there. After she left, Grandma called in her two farmer sons, her daughter-in-law and Grandpa. She told them the whole story. They just stood there with their mouths wide open.

The boys said, "We can just imagine how you must have felt when we were telling you what we did to that Jew boy. We could've sworn you weren't Jewish. What a good job you've done. Boy, are you smart."

I was relieved to come out of hiding at last. I could be a person now and be accepted for what I was – a Catholic, and no more a Jew. How often I had wished that I hadn't been a Jew because of all the persecutions the Jews had suffered.

Grandma very wisely said, "Let's not say anything to the villagers about this, not even to the uncles and their families. We'll make an appointment with the priest and tell him all about it, and everything will be fine."

We all agreed with her.

Meanwhile, we went on with our usual chores, everyone doing what he was supposed to do. After about two months the other two sons – the accountant

Paula Agauas

and the veterinarian – came for a visit. Naturally they were told everything. Everyone agreed not to wait too much longer, but that I should soon be taken to the priest to be baptized. I was comforted to know that the following Sunday we would be talking with the priest.

Saturdays were always very busy days for us. The farmers took what vegetables and fruit they'd grown, besides milk, butter, eggs and other things to the open market in the city to sell. I was usually left at home to cook potatoes for the pigs and to do all the other household chores.

On the Saturday before the Sunday we were to visit with the priest, I was left all alone as usual. In the late afternoon, after my chores were done, I sat myself by the window to knit some socks. When I looked out the window, there came that Russian and this time with my other sister, Genia.

I got so scared I could have jumped to the ceiling. There was no time to hide. They opened the door and said, "You're coming with us, for you're not safe here."

I said to the Russian, "I told you and Hannah when you were here the first time that I don't want to be a Jew. I want to be a Catholic. Why have you brought Genia here to take me away?"

My sister then said, "Have you forgotten what your father said to you? That after the war you were to go to the United States? There you'll find his sister in Detroit, and she'll be like a mother to you?"

I replied, "I haven't forgotten, but I've decided to stay here. Tomorrow I'm going to be baptized."

Upon hearing my statement Genia cried out angrily, "We've come just in time!" They grabbed me, took me to the horse and buggy, tied me inside the

Needle in a Haystack

buggy and took off with me screaming.

They brought me to the village where the widow woman lived. She and her children appeared anxious to see me. I admit that I too was excited, even though I had to be kidnapped to be brought there.

The first thing the children said to me was, "Remember, Paula, how we got on our bed and started jumping while you were hiding behind the stove? And when the villagers came in demanding to know where all of you were, we told them you weren't here? We're sorry your father got beaten up, but we couldn't help that. Even so, weren't we smart?"

With a smile, I answered, "You sure were smart, very smart." Then we all hugged and kissed each other.

Now, with my eyes full of tears, I turned to their mother and begged her, "Would you please talk to my sister, Genia, for I'm not able to get through to her. You see, I don't want to be Jewish anymore. I want to become a Catholic. Just before they kidnapped me, I was going to be baptized. Then I'd be a true Catholic. Won't you please have her take me back to Grandma and Grandpa?"

My sister and the Russian kept on trying to reason with me. "You know, even if we allowed you to go through with the baptism, the Poles will still look upon you as being a Jew and not a Catholic. Jews will *always* be persecuted. Therefore, your life will always be in danger. Don't you think the best thing for you to do is to be what you were born to be – a *Jew*?"

The mother then said to my sister, "Genia, maybe we're sinning against God by forcing her to be Jewish." But Genia just ignored her.

By then it was time for us to sit down and eat. As

we were eating, I said to Genia, "There are only three of us left alive now. It's hard for me to believe that Joseph and Father are dead." Such thoughts made me start to cry, and my appetite left me.

Then Genia said to me, "Paula, before Hannah and I left for Germany, Father came to see us. He must have expected us to help you, because the first thing he said upon entering the house was, 'Where's Paula? Isn't she here?'

"We replied to him, 'No, she isn't here. We told her to do what you had instructed her to do.'

"He moaned, 'I have killed my little daughter.' Then he fainted. When we reassured him that you were safe, he felt somewhat better and left. After that we didn't see him again, because we went to Germany."

The supper-table conversation was over. We got ready to leave for Siedlec. We arrived there to find my other sister very happy that their mission had been successful. Then she explained to me that the Jews who did come back to Siedlec felt unsafe living in separate quarters. Therefore, they had all decided to live in a kibbutz (commune). That way they'd be safe from any attack.

Since there were not enough Jews to form a kibbutz in Siedlec, they made the decision to go to Warsaw where there was a kibbutz already formed. In that kibbutz they shared everything. Nothing belonged to any one person.

When my sisters brought me to the kibbutz, I was the youngest one there. Hardly any children had survived the war, except those of families who lived in Russia. I was everyone's lost sister. My sisters had no chance. Everyone spoiled me rotten.

Needle in a Haystack

At the same time, I had to be watched very closely for they feared I might escape and go to church. Before I went to sleep, I crossed myself, knelt down by my bed and prayed. I also crossed myself before every meal.

Appointed to me as a steady baby sitter was a beautiful young woman. She had only one leg because her other leg was lost when the first bombs fell on Poland. She lived through the war in Poland, because she was hidden by a Gentile Polish family. This young woman's responsibility was to make sure I didn't run away to the Catholic Church.

She led me to the different outdoor parks. As we walked, she said, "I wish I could see you when you're all grown up. You're very good looking now, but I can see that you'll be beautiful when you're grown up."

However, I was very lonely. I missed my grandma, for I had lived with her for over two years. So they sent for her, and she came to see me a few times.

She was paid by a committee of Jews that were in Siedlec, 25,000 zwoty for keeping me. It was very difficult for her to accept the money. She knew if it had been known by her that I was a Jew, she wouldn't have kept me. She did admit this, but the money was given to her just the same.

I remember the first thing she bought herself with that money was a new shawl. The shawl she'd had before was stolen by the men in the underground movement. The women wore shawls on their heads when they went to church, and Grandma said, "I'll remember this shawl until I die."

The stay in the kibbutz was another way of life unfamiliar to me. There were so many people. Yet we were only one big family, with everyone caring for

52

Paula Agauas

everyone else.

The Passover holiday was now approaching. I remember how excited they all were to celebrate this after so many years of not being able to observe it.

Usually the youngest son of the family, who is able, asks the father the Manishtanas – also known as 'Feer Kashes' or 'Four Questions' – about why we celebrate this great holiday. Then the father explains why we have this wonderful celebration.

Since there was no younger boy and being the youngest in the kibbutz, I was chosen to ask the Four Questions. The oldest man there, who was actually like a father to all of us in the kibbutz, would answer.

I remember having to memorize those Four Questions in Hebrew. Everyone helped me with the Four Questions which are as follows:

Wherefore is this night distinguished from all other nights?

1) Any other night we may eat either leavened or unleavened bread, but on this night only unleavened bread?

2) All other nights we may eat any species of herbs, but this night only bitter herbs?

3) All other nights we do not dip even once, but on this night twice?

4) All other nights we eat and drink either sitting or reclining, but on this night we all recline?

I was scared, but I did OK. In a way we were observing this Passover not only because God had delivered the Jewish people from the hand of the Egyptian Pharaoh, but also because we had been delivered from another pharaoh, the one called 'Hitler.'

Needle in a Haystack

I was kidnapped from Grandma's village in 1945 (possibly in March), and I stayed in Warsaw through the summer of 1946. At that time everyone was making plans to leave for Germany with the intention of going to Israel later.

The whole kibbutz was on their way to Germany, but only German Jews were allowed to enter Germany. So the whole kibbutz said they were German Jews.

My sisters instructed me that I wasn't to say a thing when we were on the train. Because I didn't know enough German, it would be better if I said nothing. I was to pretend that I was deaf and dumb. If anyone said anything to me, my sisters would speak for me. I thought, *Well now, I'm deaf and dumb. What next?*

Nothing bothered me anymore.

Chapter 7
Sign Language

We arrived safely in Germany and were placed in Displaced Persons (D.P.) Camps. Not long after our arrival, I got desperately sick with an appendix attack. I was taken to a hospital and had an operation just in time. I remember being very afraid of the German doctors. I thought, *Once they get me on the operating table, I'll be dead.* I was in such pain that I was out of my head and called the doctors, "Hitlers!" But I survived. I came out of the hospital just in time to attend my sister Genia's wedding.

There were a lot of families that came back from Russia after the war. I was very happy to see them for they had children my age. There were some orphans there too that survived the war, because their parents paid Polish families all they had in order to save their lives. The parents knew that it would've been impossible for them to survive alone. It sure felt good having a girlfriend and other friends my age. I didn't feel so alone.

It didn't take long before a school was formed in the camp for us. Our teacher was a man. I remember the first morning when we enrolled, he started talking to us in Hebrew. We looked at him, thinking that he was off his rocker. We said to one another, "What's he saying? He sure is jabbering away," and we all laughed.

He stopped talking, and we stopped laughing. He proceeded to explain to us in three different languages – Jewish, Polish and Russian – to make us all understand why he spoke a language that we didn't understand. He said, "From now on you'll all speak one

Needle in a Haystack

language, and that language will be Hebrew. This is the language you just heard me speak, and I heard you laugh at it. You don't know it but this is our original language, and it'll be revived. When Israel becomes a nation, you'll speak Hebrew and no other language."

He picked up a book which contained the five books – Books of Moses – and said, "This is going to be your textbook. We have no other. You'll not only learn the language from it but also what it contains. Of course, I'll teach it to you in Hebrew, and you'll speak Hebrew in this room."

We all looked at each other without saying a word for he meant what he said. Every so often he'd interject a word for our understanding, but believe it or not, in one month we were able to write, read and even converse some in Hebrew.

Many people think that Hebrew is the same as Jewish, but it's not true. The two languages are as different as night and day. The Jewish language is more like German.

In 1947 a representative from the Hagana (Freedom Fighters) came to the camp to prepare some of the children to be smuggled into Israel. I spoke enough Hebrew to teach the kindergarten children in that camp. When the Hagana representative said to me that I'd be doing the same thing in Israel, and that I was needed there, of course I wanted to go.

I told my sisters and they didn't object to my going, for I was a real fighter, ready to fight for a land that would belong to us. We wouldn't be persecuted in the world for we'd have our own nation, and I wouldn't have to fear anyone anymore!

I got my suitcase, packed the few things I had into

Paula Agauas

it and left with a bunch of other boys and girls for the truck. We all got on the truck, drove to the gate and stopped there for inspection. A friend of my brother-in-law was on duty at the time. He noticed me, dragged me off the truck and told the driver to move on.

He tried to explain to me how dangerous it was to go. He said that it'd be a miracle if they arrived in Israel safely. Sure enough, after a month or so we heard that the whole group was killed by a bomb after they arrived in Israel.

After such reports, some of the people started to lose sight of going to Israel and began to register to go to other countries: Argentina, Brazil, Canada, France, or anywhere a country would take them in. No one could really blame them after all they'd gone through.

My brother-in-law had a family in New York. They sent him and my sister papers to go there. They wanted to take me with them but couldn't. In order for me to be able to go with them, they registered me with other orphans who were to go to the United States of America (USA). An American social worker arrived at the D.P. camp to register all the children without parents that wanted to go to America.

It sounded good to my sister, but my heart was set for Israel especially when my Hebrew was coming along so good. I just hated the thought of having to learn another language - English.

After already speaking Jewish, Polish, Russian, German and Hebrew, I was beginning to speak Czechoslovakian and Hungarian. I seemed to have no problem picking up a language. But English sounded very hard to me. I thought that I'd have to pop a hot potato in my mouth in order to get the proper sound.

Needle in a Haystack

Shortly after I was registered, I was interviewed a few times and then was taken away by a worker in a Jeep to a children's center which was also in Germany. The children's center was more like a resort. We were there for a few months until we gained some weight. Then we were taken to a larger center near Munich.

This children's center consisted of children from different parts of the world. They were waiting for their visas, like I was, for the USA. The buildings were divided into dorms. One block consisted of boys and another of girls. They were staffed with room mothers.

We each had a choice of different trades to study. School started at 9:00 a.m. and lasted till 4:00 p.m. I studied to be a dental technician which was very interesting. Another girl and I were the only ones in the class with a bunch of boys. The German professor we had was really nice.

One day I received a letter from my sister telling me that her husband changed his mind about going to the USA. Rather he wanted to go to his own country, now that we had a country.

It was in 1948 that Israel was declared a nation. I'll never forget it. Everyone danced the 'Hora' in the streets. What joy was in the camp! We had all registered before that, and I left for the children's center in Germany after Israel was declared a nation.

I couldn't see why my brother-in-law even changed his mind. It puzzled me. In her letter my sister went on to say that they were already packed and on the way. She told me that they'd be stopping within the vicinity where the children's center was, and that I'd be able to come and see them off. At the same time it would be arranged for me to leave for Israel.

I met them at the appointed place. There were others who were very enthusiastic and who tried to talk me into going to Israel. They even had someone there waiting to take me to the airplane so I could be in Israel before they were.

I got excited and said, "Yes." But I forgot that I left the children's center without permission. So I told my sister about it.

She told me, "Just go back before they notice you're missing. Don't tell them anything about the plans we've just made. If they find out, you'll not be able to leave."

I said, "OK," and left with the intention of sneaking out from the children's center the following day and flying to Israel.

When I arrived at camp it was supper time, but I wasn't too hungry. I went to the cafeteria, and who approached me but the Rabbi! The first thing he said was, "Where were you this afternoon? I looked, but you were nowhere around."

I thought to myself, *I have to talk to someone that I can trust, and why should I not trust the Rabbi?* So I told him everything.

He looked at me and said, "They all mean well, but you're still so young. You've never really lived. You go to the USA and experience what it's like to live as a normal person.

"Go to school with children that have never gone through what you've gone through, and learn. After you've been there for awhile, you can always go to Israel. But it won't be so easy to go to the USA from Israel."

Needle in a Haystack

When he was through talking, I remembered what Father said. "After the war go to America." I told this to the Rabbi.

He said, "Do what you heard your father say and don't listen to anyone else."

I didn't even go back to tell them that I wasn't going to Israel. I stayed right there and went to school until my visa was ready for me to leave for the USA.

On September 22, 1949, I left Munich, Germany by plane with other teenagers who were going to America. The only ones allowed on the plane were children and pregnant women from D.P. camps. Husbands were to follow by boat, because there wasn't room for them on the plane.

Even though we were a little scared, we were all quite excited about the plane ride as it was the first time for us. The ride was really nice until I went into the restroom and saw one of the pregnant women vomiting. I felt real good up to that time! After that I had to constantly have a bag at my seat. I was so nauseous. I would never have made it to the restroom again.

Our first landing was in Ireland. I remember we were taken to a beautiful restaurant for supper. The tables were elegantly set with waiters and waitresses serving us. It was a beautiful sight for everyone, but I was too sick to enjoy it. I was the only one that was sick.

I surely had mixed emotions when it came time to board the plane again, but I had no choice. The second landing took place in Newfoundland. There we were taken for some refreshments, probably while the plane was being refueled. From there our destination was America.

60

Paula Agauas

Chapter 8
Foster Parents

We landed in New York where a representative from the Jewish Social Service was awaiting us. We were all taken to a children's center where food was waiting for us. It was a completely new atmosphere. Somehow, we managed to go to sleep after being up for hours.

We awakened for breakfast, and after breakfast we were instructed as to what they were going to do with us. We were each told where we were going from there.

I was told that as soon as they could find a foster home for me in Detroit, I would be sent there. I didn't want to go to Detroit. I wanted to go with my girlfriend to St. Paul, Minnesota. They said, "We've been searching for your aunt. You've told us that your father said he has a sister there. We ran ads in the papers, and no one's answered them. We've decided to send you there. By being in the same city, it might be easier for you to find her. That's why you're going there."

Two weeks after Yom Kippur I was put on a train going to Detroit. When I arrived a Jewish social worker met me and took me to her office. From there she called the foster parents informing them of my safe arrival. Shortly afterwards we arrived at their home.

They sure picked a family for me! They only spoke English and not a word of anything else. You can just imagine how I felt. You'd think that the social worker would've had some understanding of my feelings. If only she would have just realized how forlorn I felt, for I didn't know anyone.

At least she could've placed me with a family that

61

Needle in a Haystack

spoke one of the languages I was familiar with, but instead she concentrated on a family that was Jewish. I, of course, thought that every Jew in the world spoke Jewish. In Poland we spoke Polish and Jewish. So when I was asked what kind of family I wanted to live with, Jewish Orthodox or Conservative, I told them, "One not so religious."

However, I didn't know that there could be Jews in America that didn't know a word of Jewish. I took it for granted that they'd all speak Jewish and English. Even though I was unfamiliar with such Jews, they weren't even Reformed Jews. After awhile I found out that most American Jews were Jews by name only.

The social worker took me there and introduced me to Mr. and Mrs. Whispy, a son, a daughter the same age as I, and a young man who was a boarder. Again I began speaking sign language, but this time I didn't have to be deaf and dumb as on the train from Poland to Germany. The social worker said, "I'll let you stay here for a few days, and after that I'll come back and take you to a school where you'll learn English."

After staying with the foster parents for about six months, somehow my foster mother found out about a club where only people of Siedlec met. She told me about it, and I thought it'd be very interesting for me to meet them. I expressed my feelings to her.

She said, "I'll get the telephone number from the president of the club. I'll inform her of your being with us. Maybe she'll be able to come over and meet you."

Of course, I got real excited, and told her to get in touch with her, thinking maybe my father's sister meets with them.

I couldn't wait to meet this woman. The time came

Paula Agauas

for her to come over one evening. She was a very pleasant person to talk to. I told her about my family, and she knew them all from Poland. She especially knew my mother and told me how beautiful and talented she was. But she didn't know of my aunt here in America, let alone in Detroit.

I told her that even from Germany they had looked for her in all the papers. So she said, "I bet they didn't look for her in the 'Forvertz' (Jewish paper). She probably doesn't read English. Many of those people, even though they've been here for years, have never learned to read and write English.

"I'll tell you what I'll do. I'll go to the Forvertz and tell them about you and your aunt. They'll have a write-up about this in the Forvertz. If she's still alive, you can be sure to hear from her."

As soon as that was done, I heard from that woman president on the telephone telling me that a woman answering that description called the Forvertz. You can just imagine what went through my mind. She said, "Tomorrow morning they'll have this woman in their office, and you be ready for I'm picking you up to meet her."

I hardly slept that night, and everyone in that household was excited with me. The following morning I got up, ate breakfast and off we went to the Forvertz.

Everyone in that place stopped working, and they were all gathered in one area to witness the reunion. I couldn't imagine how in the world I'd know if she was really my aunt. As I was approaching the group of people, my eyes caught this woman's eyebrows. They looked just like my father's! I walked right up to her and said, "You're my father's sister."

Needle in a Haystack

She said, "How do you know?"

"By your eyebrows," I said. "They're just like Father's." Then she sat down with me and had me describe Father and the rest of the family.

In the meantime, all the people there were just standing with their mouths wide open, not wanting to miss one word. After a while she said to all, "This is really my niece. There's no doubt about it. I looked in that paper ever since the war was over, hoping someone by that name would be in the paper. Every day I saw everyone looking for someone else, not knowing if anyone was left alive from my family. Now, after all this, I saw my maiden name in the paper."

Of course she was married, and her name was not the same. After that I found that I had a first cousin, her daughter, and cousins in New York and Argentina.

I moved out from the foster parents' home to live with my aunt. Her home was just like ours back in Poland – strictly Jewish Orthodox and not at all like an American Jew. She was here, but the atmosphere was of Poland. Under all that law!

I wasn't used to that kind of life anymore, and my aunt knew it. So she called me the 'shikse' (Gentile). When it came Saturday, I was able to turn on the stove or a light because I wasn't like her.

I took a knife by mistake one time that was supposed to have been used for meats only. I used it for butter, and she saw it. That knife was polluted after that. She took the knife and put it in the ground for twenty-four hours and then scrubbed it. This is the way it had to be purified under the law. After that incident, I had to be very careful.

I thought that when I found my aunt, I'd be able to

Paula Agauas

live with her, and that it would be like my father had said. "She'll be like a mother to you." But after I moved in with her, I found it to be more of a shock to me than when I came to the foster home.

After being with my aunt for a while, I wondered which was worse. There I didn't know the language, but here I was completely out of touch with this Jewish Orthodox way of living. We had to have two sets of dishes, two sets of silverware, two sets of dish towels, and remember not to eat dairy foods for six hours after having eaten meat. Don't turn on a light after sundown on Friday, or light the stove or answer the telephone through sundown Saturday.

My aunt lived in one of the apartment houses on Gladstone, right off Twelfth Street. Her first husband had died, and she was remarried. The man she was married to now was very nice and so humble. He worked for a synagogue. They weren't poor and they weren't rich, but they had a contentment about them. They liked things just as they were.

The Americanization school was only a block away from where my aunt lived. I had to take a street car when I lived on Martindale Street with the foster parents. So it worked out real well.

One Friday before the sun went down, my aunt sent me to the bakery for a chalah (egg bread). The traffic was very heavy at that hour, so cars stopped to let me cross the street. But one car at the other end didn't see me. It was coming at full speed. I still believe this was a miracle that I wasn't killed. I ran across with such a force that I was lucky there was a wall to run into to stop me. The cars just kept honking and honking at that man. I was safe again!

The time came for me to enter regular classes. I

65

Needle in a Haystack

was put with the ninth graders. I liked it very much. In order for me to make up a full grade, I went to summer school. While in summer school, I met a girl who became my friend. She didn't live too far from me, so we used to be in each other's homes quite often.

Paula Agauas

Chapter 9
Rubin

One of the boys who was sent to Chicago from the children's center found out where I lived from a friend he was visiting in Detroit. He called me and asked if I'd like to go swimming. His friend had a car and would like to meet me. "If you have a friend for me, I'd like to meet her, and the four of us can go swimming at Rouge Park."

It all sounded so nice. I told him, "But I can't go out because of all the homework I have." He pleaded with me until I said "Yes." I told him, "Please call me back for I have to call my girlfriend, Martha."

I called her, and there was no problem, but she said, "My cousin, Rubin, has a date. How about them coming with us since he doesn't have a car?"

"The more the merrier," I said.

They arrived, and it was nice to see my friend from the children's center once more. He introduced me to his friend, and we were soon on our way to pick up Martha and her cousin.

We honked the horn for Martha to come out. I didn't know that her cousin, Rubin, lived right next door to her. As he came out, I looked at him and said to myself, "I'd like to marry this man." Then I thought, *I must be insane thinking such things.*

The girl he was taking out lived next door to Martha too. We all got in the car and off we went to Rouge Park. The weather was beautiful. As we were swimming, I forgot that I really didn't know how to swim. I was underwater having a great time when

Needle in a Haystack

someone swam under me and lifted me up bodily. Who was it but Rubin Agauas!

After that, we were inseparable. This girl gave Rubin a birthday party, and he invited me to be his guest. In the middle of the party, he grabbed my hand. We ran off to the park, with everyone else following us. It was a riot. In short, we were in love. You might call it love at first sight.

Shortly after, he enlisted in the Merchant Marines. I didn't hear from him for a while, but after a few months he wrote me a letter. So we corresponded. Then he was drafted into the Army. In the meantime, I was going to school and finishing my high school education.

I had many friends. Boys were no problem. I went to parties and loved to dance. I couldn't see going any place where there was no dancing. Rubin didn't really dance, but he did a slow tango. I couldn't see myself being married to anyone that didn't know how to dance.

Staying with my aunt was becoming very difficult due to her set ways. I told my social worker that I'd like to move out. She found me a foster home, and I moved with my aunt's consent for she understood me. By this time I was able to make myself understood by my social worker, for language wasn't a barrier any more.

Therefore she was able to find me a foster home that fitted more to my heart's desire. They were a middle-aged Jewish couple living alone. They had one daughter who was married and away from home. They spoke some Jewish, but then it didn't matter to me anymore.

Rubin came home from the Army after being stationed in Germany. That was March of 1953. We became engaged, and at the same time I was finishing high school. We decided to get married June 28, 1953.

Paula Agauas

It was a very exciting time! On June 17th I graduated, and on the 28th we were married in a Jewish Orthodox Synagogue with Cantor Adler singing 'Because.'

I worked for Twentieth Century Fox Film Corporation doing general office work, mostly typing. I became pregnant after the doctor said that I wouldn't be able to have any children. On June 17, 1955, Nathan Jeffrey Agauas was born. He was so ugly that he was beautiful. When I'd take him for a walk in the buggy, I'd put him on his stomach so no one would see him. But as he got older, he got better looking.

Rubin loved me so much that he wanted to give me everything to make me happy. One thing stopped him, and that thing was money. In order to obtain money quickly, he began to gamble. The more he played the cards, the more he lost even to the point of losing the rent money.

Nathan was only six months old at that time. Not having anyone to help me, I was unable to work. Rubin would stay out for nights at a time. He'd show up in the morning but with no money!

Things were getting desperate with us. I wanted to divorce him. But each time I'd think about it, I'd remember what the Rabbi said. "Whom God has joined together, let no man put asunder." I'd get this terrible fear of God, and because of it I couldn't go through with it. There was no way out.

One morning while Nathan was having his nap, I laid myself down on the couch with the television on. Instead of watching it, I was trying to decide what would be the easiest way to commit suicide. I felt that no one cared if I were alive or dead. The only time I had a husband, family and friends was when I was able to entertain them and give them extravagant gifts.

Chapter 10
Jesus – the Messiah

As I was meditating on these unpleasant things and forgetting even that the TV was on, I heard the announcer say, "If you feel that you're all alone and no one cares for you, remember, God loves you." I awakened from my thoughts and became very quiet, as if every fiber in my being was overcome with a perfect peace.

In this attitude of mind, I heard these words being spoken in me. "Don't you remember when I was with you when you were all alone, and I cared for you? I am Jesus, and I am with you now."

I didn't have to hear anything else. I jumped off the couch and screamed, "Jesus, Jesus. You're still in my heart. You never left me, and I thought that no one cared for me. Oh how I love you, Jesus."

I could hardly contain myself. I felt as if I owned the whole world! After a little while I sat down and thought of all that had been transpiring in this short time. All of a sudden my thoughts came into focus. "What am I doing? I'm not supposed to believe in Jesus anymore. I'm a Jew. I'm sinning against God. I'm not going to tell a soul about it. I'll just keep it to myself."

I got my thoughts together, straightened up the place and began dinner. Rubin came home from work, and all was well. That is, as well as could be, for Rubin still gambled. But I never was the same after that experience. Somehow, I wasn't as lonely as before.

The holidays – Rosh Hashana and Yom Kippur (the Day of Atonement) – were approaching. Everyone whose parents, brother or sister were deceased usually

Paula Agauas

went to the synagogue to say Yizkor, a prayer for that person on that day.

Rubin and I went to the synagogue to say this prayer, but they wouldn't let us in because we didn't buy a ticket. I just couldn't believe my ears. I couldn't go into the house of God without paying for a ticket?

Some of our friends came out of the synagogue and offered to give us their tickets so we could go in to say that prayer. But I wouldn't hear of it. I told them that I knew a God that hears me without having to pay for a ticket to enter the synagogue. I asked Rubin to take me home.

After a few weeks I became very concerned about Nathan. I remembered how Father would sit down with my brother and me and have us repeat after him the daily prayers. But Rubin didn't even read the Bible and was not at all like my father. How would our child learn about God when Rubin hadn't read a thing about God since he had to memorize some of the things from the Torah for his Bar Mitzvah? I became panicky. Yet, I couldn't do a thing about it but ponder it all in my heart.

Weeks went by when suddenly someone knocked at the door. I opened it with the chain still on the door, for Rubin told me to keep the door latched and let no stranger in. It was a man saying he was just taking a survey. He asked me if I belonged to a synagogue or church.

I said, "No, I don't belong to anything like that, but I've been thinking a lot about our son. I'm wondering how he's going to learn about the things of God when his father doesn't know the Bible."

I realized that the man was still behind the door.

Needle in a Haystack

So I unchained the door and was able to see that the man looked Jewish. I asked him if he was Jewish. The answer, of course, was "Yes."

He said, "I believe that Jesus is the Messiah."

I had him repeat that statement. I never heard of another Jew believing in Jesus, and here is a Jew that tells me that he believes that Jesus was the Messiah!

I couldn't contain myself. I told him about what happened to me a few months ago previous to his coming, when I was lying on the couch. I also told him what I was told when I looked at the picture of Jesus many years before.

So he opened the Bible to John 16:33 and read this to me: *"These things I have spoken unto you, that in me ye might have peace. In the world ye shall have tribulation: but be of good cheer; I have overcome the world."*

I had to read it for myself. I couldn't believe that he was really reading it. Sure enough, there it was in black and white. I jumped off the chair with excitement. The same Jesus that I knew as just another Jew is the very Messiah! I hardly could contain it.

Of course, he had to leave for it was getting late. I told him that I could hardly wait for my husband to come from work so that I could tell him this wonderful news. I asked him to come over in the evening so my husband could meet him. He said he would come with his wife. Then he left.

Rubin came from work shortly after he left, and I ran up to him and kissed him (which I hadn't done in a long time). He didn't know what got in me and asked what I had been drinking.

I said, "This man was here and told me that Jesus is the Messiah, and he too is a Jew. You see, for the longest time I thought that I was sinning because I believed in Jesus, but I would never tell you about it. Today I found out that He's the Messiah. Isn't that wonderful?"

Rubin got red in his face and said, "You're crazy! I don't want you to mention this to anyone, and you better forget about this whole thing."

I didn't say a thing after that to him and began to serve supper.

Rubin also was born into a Jewish Orthodox home, the youngest of five boys. His father so longed for a girl that I can just imagine how he really must have felt after being disappointed for the fifth time. On top of all that, Rubin's mother died from childbirth when she had Rubin.

Rubin grew up with the thought in his mind that his father always resented him for it, for he would be harshly disciplined by his father. His father would accuse him of doing things that he'd never even think of doing. He always called Rubin a liar. It came to the place that he thought to himself, *I might as well do some of the things he's accusing me of doing, then I'll at least feel a little better.*

Rubin didn't have a home life, and he was mostly brought up by his aunts. His father remarried when Rubin was about twelve years old. Things got better for him since he had a more normal home.

After Rubin's mother died, his father gave up his belief – even in the existence of a God – for he had loved her very much. I might say that he became an atheist. But I liked him a lot, and I was his favorite

Needle in a Haystack

daughter-in-law.

He would say to me, "Paula, I like you for you always tell me the truth. You're not like my other daughters-in-law. They say one thing to me, and behind my back they would stab me. Why are you marrying my Rubin? You can get yourself someone much better."

So I told him, "Because I love him." Then he'd laugh. He was a very honest person and could make a dollar stretch farther than anyone I knew.

Here's something really funny. Every time it got windy outside, he'd call me up and say, "Paula, don't go out today."

I'd ask, "Why?"

He'd reply, "The wind will blow you away." (I weighed ninety-five pounds and was five feet tall.) Or he'd say. "Don't eat spaghetti for you're too short."

When Nathan was born I was going to name him Joseph, but when I awakened from the anesthetic Rubin told me that I wouldn't be able to name him Joseph. So I asked him, "Why?"

He said, "Because my father is still alive."

I was disappointed for I wanted our son named after my brother, Joseph. So Nathan was named after my father, but I nicknamed him 'Neddy.'

Nathan was our only child to have a grandpa and a grandma. He was deeply loved by them. Grandpa spoiled him for four years. One evening while Grandpa was watching wrestling on television, he said to his wife, "Would you please get me a glass of water. I don't feel so good." While she was in the kitchen getting the water, he died of a heart attack in the chair. The man was never really sick in his lifetime.

Paula Agauas

A year later I gave birth to our second son. I was disappointed that he wasn't a girl. But this time I was able to name him Joseph, not only after my brother, but also after my father-in-law whom I respected very much. Joey, in a way, is like his grandfather for he is sports crazy too.

After I told Rubin about my good news that Jesus is the Messiah, I just couldn't wait to call my cousin and tell her also. When I called her and she heard me, she gave such a scream in the telephone that I thought my eardrum would break.

She said, "If you persist in this nonsense, you'll never hear from me!" She hung up without saying good-bye. After that, I didn't hear from her for a while.

After a week or so, I received a telephone call from the same man asking if it was all right for his wife and him to come over in the evening. I said, "Yes."

Rubin came home, and I told him that we were going to have company. Of course, he wanted to know who was coming over. I told him. To my surprise he didn't object.

They came and I introduced Rubin to them and right off they said, "Just call us Betty and Ted. Our last name is Paul." They were so very friendly. Rubin liked them right away. We talked about many things. Rubin liked to read comic books, so Ted began to read comic books. The next time they came over they had that in common.

Rubin felt so free talking to them that he made this remark one evening. "I have to be honest with you. When I went to see <u>The Ten Commandments</u> I thought that Charleton Heston was Moses. That's how much I know about the Bible."

Needle in a Haystack

After awhile they brought other Hebrew-Christians for us to meet. One evening Rev. Glass came over. He was the pastor of the Hebrew-Christian Church. Right away he started preaching to Rubin - not at all like Ted. Rubin literally told him to leave then opened the door for him. I just sat there with my mouth open.

After that Ted and Betty asked me to go to their church one evening for a baby shower given for Betty. She was expecting her first baby at that time. I agreed to go, and I got to meet a lot of Jewish Christians for the first time. Grace Brickner introduced herself to me. She was the daughter of Rev. Glass. I wondered if Rubin would even say hello to her after meeting her father, but I asked her to come and visit us with her husband.

It wasn't long after that until they came, and Rubin met Harold and Gracey. We became close friends. They brought over Charley Jones, who was a Gentile believer. Yet to me he seemed to be a true Jew, because he knew Jesus like I did.

Then came the time that Charley and Harold asked Rubin to go with them to the Hebrew-Christian Church to hear Haskell Stone speak. Rubin accepted the invitation.

I stayed home with the baby, Nathan, who was three years old by then. I read the Bible that Ted Paul had given me after his first visit. I just devoured the Gospel of John. To me, the book of John was the whole Bible because of John 16:33. Every page was full of love.

After that it was the Psalms of David. I just couldn't wait to partake of the 'Word of Life.' I never had to memorize scriptures. They just jumped out of the pages and into my heart.

One time Ted Paul suggested I take a scripture

memorization course published by the Navigators, and I said "OK." I tried but couldn't, no matter how hard I tried. I finally told him it was no use, and I gave it up.

As I was sitting there reading the Bible, Rubin and the others came back from church. I didn't really expect anything to happen, but I looked up at Rubin and his face looked different, full of excitement. "Honey, all my life I cursed God and didn't know it. Haskel was speaking from the book of Job. When he came to the part where Job's wife said, 'Why don't you curse God and die?' (Job 2:9), I realized right there that God was telling me that I was cursing Him. Honey, He is the Messiah!" He hugged and kissed me, but I didn't tell him that he was crazy as he had told me.

When he said, "I want to be just like Job," I got upset. He didn't really know the book of Job. I had already read it in my times of trials with him when he was giving me a hard time. He didn't know what he was asking.

So I told him, "You better not ask to be like Job right now, but read that book first and then tell me if you still want to be like him."

Rubin, of course, was very serious and said, "I don't care. I still want to be like him."

That evening we all rejoiced and sang. Rubin started to read the Bible for the first time in the same hungry way as I did. I was no longer alone in the household believing in Jesus the Messiah. I had my husband.

Rubin asked Haskell if he'd hold Bible studies in our fourth floor apartment. He was very happy to do this. So every Friday night our apartment was full of people hungry to learn the Word of God. Since the book of John was my favorite book, he started with it. Then

Needle in a Haystack

he taught on the 'Sermon on the Mount' in Matthew 5. As far as I was concerned, it was Jesus speaking from the pages to me personally, as if no one else was in the room.

After that study we got into Matthew 28 to the place of 'The Great Commission.' It was emphasized how important it is for us to be baptized. In order to become a member of the church and be obedient to that 'Word,' Rubin and I decided to be baptized.

Ted Paul baptized us in the name of the Father and the Son and the Holy Ghost. We both felt very good. I went to sleep that Sunday night and dreamed that a dove set itself on my shoulder and cuddled me with its wings. When I awakened in the morning, I could still feel the warmth of its feathers.

I remember Betty Paul mentioning to me a few times about Jesus being 'the very God.' I'd just look at her and think to myself, *She can't mean that – Jesus, God. I know him now as the Messiah, but not God.* She never argued with me.

One day Grace Brickner invited me for lunch. I went. There were only the two of us, and we were just chatting about everything. Then she made this statement. "You know, Paula, Rosalind Stone and I were talking about you the other day. We came to the conclusion that you don't know Jesus as the very God, but just as the Son of God, the Messiah."

I said, "How else should I know Him when He is that?"

Grace opened the Bible and said, "Sit down with me on the couch, and let's read Isaiah 9:6: *"For unto us a child is born, unto us a Son is given: and the government shall be upon His shoulder: and His name shall be called Wonderful, Counsellor, the Mighty God,*

78

the Everlasting Father, the Prince of Peace."

She read it the first time, but it didn't register. It was as if a veil was over my head. I was blank, and I knew it. I said to her, "I don't know what you're trying to prove." She prayed that God would take this veil away from me and reveal Himself as the very God.

Then I read it for myself, and for the first time I saw Him as God. I jumped from the couch, grabbed Grace and danced around and around. I couldn't contain myself for the great joy that flooded my being. I couldn't imagine that the Creator of the whole world and everything in it could love me personally! For the first time, He had revealed Himself to me as a personal God.

My soul escaped like a bird

Out of the snare of the fowler.

My soul escaped like a bird

Out of the snare of the fowler.

The snare is broken

And I am escaped.

My help is in the name of the Lord.

My help is in the name of the Lord.

It wasn't long after this experience that a change took place in the Hebrew-Christian Church. Quite a few of us started meeting in each other's homes every Sunday. We then truly experienced New Testament living. We just didn't come together in the morning for one or two hours, but for the whole day and evening. The word does declare, *"Man shall not live by bread alone, but by every word that proceedeth out of the*

Needle in a Haystack

mouth of God" (Matthew 4:4). So we ate of that word.

About six months later I became pregnant with Joseph Richard Agauas. We then had to look for another place to live for the apartment would've been too small for another child. I was in my fifth month when Rubin looked in the paper and found a downstairs five-room flat. I remember moving into the flat the first of April with our friends painting and getting it ready for us. We then had more room for everyone to sit around the dining room table comfortably.

Paula Agauas

Chapter 11
Blind Eyes

We that are born

Born of the King

Let's sing a new song

A new song to the King

Let's sing praises

Praises to our King

Glory Hallelujah

Jesus is the King

Good Friday came around quickly, and I was glad that we were moved before Easter. I remember the weather on that Good Friday of 1960 was just beautiful. It was in the afternoon when I asked Rubin to take Nathan and me for a ride.

As we were driving I became more nervous than usual, and suddenly I said to Rubin, "Rubin, you're making me very nervous, the way you drive. Don't you see how close you are to the other car? If he suddenly stops, you'll have no chance but to hit him. Why don't you see Dr. Benjamin, the eye doctor? You probably need glasses."

Rubin said, "All right. I've noticed lately that my eyes have been failing me. Let's stop and see him now. If he's too busy, I'll make an appointment."

We got to the office and Dr. Benjamin, knowing the family, took him in right away to have his eyes examined and fitted for glasses. I waited and waited, and finally they came out.

Needle in a Haystack

Rubin said to me, "He can't give me any glasses. He advises me to go to Sinai Hospital. There they'll run further tests on me. The doctor suspects a tumor behind my eyes and glasses won't help me."

Of course, he had to go as soon as room was available. The following Monday he was admitted and stayed there for 10 days. After 10 days they had the true results, stating all the facts. They didn't find a tumor behind his eyes or on the brain. Hearing the good news made me very happy, but not for long. Rubin said, "I have glaucoma. They'll try to operate if it isn't too late."

I had never heard of this disease. So after I left Rubin in the hospital, I went to see this eye specialist that was in charge of him to find out what was truly going on. The doctor invited me into his office. Of course he knew why I came to see him. Without an explanation, he said to me, "Mrs. Agauas, your husband is blind."

I hardly could believe my ears. So I asked him to repeat it, which he did. He explained to me that it was too late to operate, and in a matter of three or six months Rubin would have to have a white cane.

I always abhorred seeing people with white canes. I could never imagine how anyone could live that way, and now the very thing I feared came into my own life. (I was thinking this as he was talking.) I said to him, "Are you sure? Have you consulted with other doctors?"

He said, "Yes, there's no question about it." He got very angry with me, saying, "It'll take a real miracle to restore his eyes!"

That is all I had to hear. Little did he know that my being alive is a miracle. I told him, "You just gave me great hope by saying what you just said. I do believe in a

Paula Agauas

God of miracles," and I left the office. I got into the car rejoicing and crying at the same time, for I knew without a doubt that God would take care of the situation.

I was invited to my girlfriend's house for dinner that day. When I got there, she asked me what the doctor said. (She wasn't a believer.) I told her without being able to control my tears, not realizing that I was out of God's atmosphere – realm of faith – and back to the earthly atmosphere. The only thing I could see was having a blind husband! I said to Freida, "I hope and pray that he'll at least be able to see his newborn child before he goes blind."

So she cried with me and comforted me.

The following morning I went to pick Rubin up from the hospital. He asked if the doctor talked with me. I said, "Yes." I asked him what the doctor said to him.

Rubin said, "I'll have to take drops four times a day and some pills. I can go back to work and see him in two weeks."

Of course, the company Rubin worked for (American Tubing Co.) wanted a statement concerning Rubin's absence. The doctor filled out a form and sent it in. It didn't take long after that until Rubin was told that he would be unable to work there –or any other place. No one wants to take a chance on someone that's going blind. He was a bad risk. Therefore the labor union wouldn't allow him to work. And no other job was available.

We didn't know where our rent would come from or money for all the other expenses, especially with a second baby being on the way. There was a doctor's bill

Needle in a Haystack

of $100 unpaid. I'd been paying him off with each visit until Rubin lost his job. The thought of it all would make me sick to my stomach.

The first thing you would hear someone say was, "Why don't you go on welfare?" But I couldn't hear of it. I just knew that this wasn't God's will concerning us. Rubin agreed. We told the church fellowship about it. They felt the same way.

We turned to the Word to find out how the New Testament church handled a situation like this. In Acts 2:44-47 we found the answer: *"And all that believed were together...and parted to all men, as every man had need. They continuing daily with one accord, breaking bread from house to house...Praising God, and having favor with all people..."*

We weren't the only fellowship that saw this truth. There were fellowships in Colorado and in California that saw it. They, too, lived in that manner. When they found out about us, they wrote and asked if they could help. Many times they sent us money when there was a shortage in our fellowship.

Many times I'd look in my purse and find money unaccounted for. Or in the mailbox we'd find envelopes with money in them, not knowing where they came from.

One afternoon about 4:30 p.m. while we were in the back yard, the mailman brought us a special delivery letter containing a cashier's check for the amount of $100. It came just a few days before my six-week checkup after Joey was born.

I knew exactly what this check was for. It was in my name, and the balance of my doctor's bill was $100. I just took the check with me and signed it over.

Paula Agauas

This went on for two years. Every need was beautifully provided by the true and living God. That's the way we learned God as Jehovah-Jireh: *'The Lord will provide.'*

Joseph was born August 9, 1960, and Rubin's eyes could see him. Even though he was a beautiful baby Rubin was very impatient with him, because of the fear he had of being blind someday.

One day I got so angry that I told him, "Look, we have a choice. We can commit the whole thing to God and be happy knowing that all things work together for good to them that love God (Romans 8:28). Or we can go on arguing about everything, and before we know it we'll not be able to stand each other. This is all up to you."

Rubin listened, and when I was through he said, "You're absolutely right. I'm a heel! After what God has already done for us, we're going to be happy as we look to the Lord and not at the circumstances."

Not long after this conversation took place, Rubin went to a Thursday morning service and had Pastor M. D. Beall pray for his eyes. God arrested the disease so that it didn't go any further.

A social worker was assigned to Rubin from the Association of the Blind. The social worker himself was completely blind with a white cane, but he got along better than some that could see. He was a very pleasant person. He told us of the literature that the Library of the Blind had. Before long, Rubin began to receive literature for the partially blind with real large letters. The regular print was too small for him.

After a while his eyes began to get tired reading even the large print. So the library offered a selection of

Needle in a Haystack

talking records. The Bible was in this selection. Rubin had the Psalms sent first along with a record player. I was excited with him. The records were read by Alexander Scorby, a beautiful reader.

I was able to go on with my household duties and, with Rubin, listen to the Word of God being read.

I can say that for seven years we went through a school that had been prepared for us by the living God. Praise His Holy Name. What a wonderful Teacher we have.

After the two years of revealing Himself to us as a provider, we began to receive Social Security Disability checks and V. A. pension checks. This was something we never counted on. The fellowship was very happy for this door being opened to us, and everyone was thanking God for it.

But after having such beautiful fellowship in the homes, a spirit of dissension came into our group. I, for one, began to get very dissatisfied. I wanted more of God. I didn't know what to think of it. I heard myself saying, "I have to come out of this."

Paula Agauas

Chapter 12
The Holy Spirit

Everyone in the group knew Mr. and Mrs. Walter Wilson. They had us call them 'Uncle Scoop and Aunt Dot.' They lived around the corner from us. One day Aunt Dot asked me if I'd be willing to go the next Sunday morning to give my testimony to her Sunday school class at the Bethesda Missionary Temple. I didn't know what to say, so I told her that I'd tell the group about it and see what they had to say.

On Friday as usual, everyone came to the Bible study which was at our house. After we all sat down, I told them about Aunt Dot asking me to give my testimony to her class. I asked if they'd pray about it with me, for I wanted God's will.

It was quiet for a little while, and then Haskell said, "I don't see why you shouldn't go, but you might not be the same afterwards. You know, they have a woman preacher there."

I had never heard of a woman preacher before. Dot had never told me before either, but why should she have told me? She only asked me to come to her class.

Then another one said, "I don't think she should go. As far as I know Paula, she'll leave our group and like it there."

I couldn't understand why they talked like that. So I said, "What are you saying? I could never leave you."

She laughed and said, "You'll see if I'm wrong." After that nothing else was said.

Sunday morning came, and it was our turn to have everyone at our house. They came and, of course, I was

Needle in a Haystack

asked if I was going.

I said, "Yes."

They said that they'd positively pray for me.

The Wilsons came and picked me up. They introduced me to the supervisors of their department, Mr. and Mrs. Hoffman, who seemed to be nice people, and then to the other teachers who were very pleasant. After the children got to their classes, Sunday school began. Dot's class never heard such a testimony before, and you could've heard a pin drop.

As soon as the class was over, Dot couldn't wait to get me out of there to the main service without telling me about it. The building was packed that Sunday morning. But she and Scoop didn't hesitate to take me all the way to the front saying, "We don't want you to miss a thing."I think we sat in the second row which didn't make me feel too comfortable, but it didn't last for long.

The service started with singing and with this I was familiar, but then the clapping of the hands began which was unfamiliar to me. Yet I didn't resent it. I liked it and clapped with them. Then the song leader said, "Let's all enter into praise," and they all began to praise God.

I had to look through the congregation to make sure that I wasn't in a synagogue. I could have sworn that they worshiped God with the same sound. And the church didn't look to me like a church but a mere place where God's people got together to worship Him in unity.

The praise was so united – as one voice and yet about 3000 voices in one. It reminded me of that song, 'Oh for a thousand tongues to sing.'

Paula Agauas

Then this woman preacher began to preach. Being warned of her, I had mixed emotions. But I couldn't believe what came out of her mouth. Listening to her, I didn't see a woman preacher but a voice of God. Especially when I heard her say, *"Come out from among them and be ye separate, saith the Lord* (2 Corinthians 6:17)." I thought that God spoke only to me. And now I heard another woman hear from God as I did.

When I heard her say, "Come out from among them," I thought that my ear drums were going to burst. Then I thought to myself, *How did she know what I have been thinking lately?* As I was sitting there I heard myself saying, *"My sheep hear my voice, but a stranger will they not follow* (John 10:3-5)."

The service was over, and Dot and Scoop asked how I liked it. I told them how this place reminded me of a synagogue, and they laughed. I got home and told them the same thing, and that I liked this woman pastor. I didn't see any difference for I heard God speak through her to me. And that was it. No more questions.

We continued with the meetings, but sure enough it wasn't the same. There was a change in me. A terrible restlessness set in, in my spirit. I think it was on a Wednesday night or Thursday, a few of us went to the November Seminar that was being held at Bethesda.

I remember Rev. Green was speaking about the baptism of the Holy Spirit. As far as I was concerned, I was already baptized. When I told the group about this dove sitting on my shoulder, they told me that's what it was. They pointed to the place where the same thing happened to Jesus when He was baptized in the Jordan River (Matthew 3:16). After reading that account, I had no questions about it.

Needle in a Haystack

I heard Rev. Green refer to Acts, chapter two, about how the 120 people were filled with the Spirit, and they spoke in different tongues. Then he pointed to Cornelius' household in Acts, chapter 10, and I began to question the whole thing.

He then closed his message by asking, "Who among you is questioning the baptism of the Holy Spirit?"

My hand went up like a shot. I think that I was the only one, for he told us to come forward. I went forward and stood with my face to the platform wall and started talking to God. I couldn't imagine myself speaking with an unknown tongue.

After a little while I heard Dot coming up with Patricia Gruits. They began to pray with me. As they were praying, I still said, "How can this be?" But not for long! I suddenly became very quiet.

Patricia said, "The anointing is all over her. She's being baptized with the Holy Ghost."

As she was saying this, without being able to see my face, I began to whisper in a language I had never spoken before. I turned and saw more than the two there. I just loved them so much that I couldn't refrain from hugging them. Yet I didn't know any of these people but Aunt Dot.

The love of God overshadowed me. I could see a great river that had been stopped by some obstruction for a long time. But all of a sudden, it erupted and had to gush out. Nothing could stop it because of this mighty force.

We went home to get some sleep. I arose in the morning and wasn't too satisfied because I still just whispered and was unable to express orally. I went

90

about doing what had to be done. Then when the house was quiet, I entered the bedroom, closed the door and knelt down by my bed.

I asked God to enable me to speak this heavenly language clearly, and then I waited. It didn't take long – I think about a minute – that this river came forth. I not only spoke, but sang in this language. I had no more questions after that. Praise His holy name!

There is liberty in Jesus

That no man can understand.

But if they come to Jesus

They will be led by His right hand.

For it is He that leadeth thee

Through every path to liberty.

It didn't take too long after that until our group was breaking up. It was decided to have meetings during the week, but the Sunday meetings were being dropped, except for only a few that were still meeting on Sunday. And we were part of that few until the Easter convention at Bethesda.

When the Wilsons asked Rubin if he'd like to go with them to one of the meetings during the week, Rubin said, "Yes." They picked him up on Monday morning. He came home, and he was all lit up with excitement, telling me that he was going to go with them for the rest of the week.

In the middle of the week he heard Rev. McAllister from Toronto. God spoke through this man to Rubin in such a way that he had no doubt that God wanted us there. After Rubin came home that day he said, "Honey,

Needle in a Haystack

you're right. God wants us there."

I said, "It's up to you."

The meetings were over. Sunday came, and we all got ready to be on time for Sunday school. Our first Sunday school experience was in the young-married class. Herb Moos was the teacher. The first lesson was on water baptism. For some reason Rubin was irritated because of the way Herb presented the lesson.

I asked Rubin, "Why are you angry?"

He said, "He makes you feel as if you weren't baptized."

"Why should it bother you?" I said. "You know we were baptized."

After that everything was fine until a few Sundays later. Then Herb taught about water baptism again, but not exactly in the same way. When he said that one must be baptized into the name of Jesus Christ and not the Father, Son and Holy Ghost, I got angry.

Rubin asked me, "What's the matter with you?" I told him that I couldn't wait till the class was over so I could talk to Herb.

When the class was over, I asked Brother Moos, "What do you do with a person that God baptized with the Holy Ghost after they were baptized into the Triune God?"

He turned to Acts, chapter 10, to the scripture describing what happened at Cornelius' house, and how afterward they were all baptized into Christ. I thought to myself, *Yes, they were all Gentiles and that sign had to be given to Peter by God. Otherwise Peter wouldn't have seen that God showed no partiality.*

After that conversation, I was fully satisfied that

Paula Agauas

God had already done the work. Rubin and I went down to the main service. A prophecy came forth from the platform: "Sing, Oh barren, thou that didst not bear, break forth into singing," and so on (Isaiah 54:1).

I couldn't contain myself and began to cry and cry. I tried to stop but couldn't. Rubin then whispered to me, "What's the matter with you?"

I said, "I don't know. I have to get out of here. I can't stop crying.

During that week we had some of the people in our group over for an evening get-together. We sat around the table having some refreshments and sharing God's goodness. One person suggested having a time of prayer around the table. We agreed. I had no intention to pray, but as we began to sing and then go into prayer, I felt different. I heard myself asking God to cut away this stony heart and give me a heart of flesh (Ezekiel 11:19).

Everyone left. We all went to bed, but I couldn't fall asleep. I asked myself, "Why did I pray like that? I already had that done when I was baptized, and yet I prayed like the work wasn't yet done."

The Lord was reminding me about his discourse with Nicodemus about the new birth (John 3:1-5). I can't enter the kingdom of God unless I'm baptized in the name of Jesus Christ (Acts 2:38), and no other name (Acts 4:12) for in Him rests the Godhead bodily (Colossians 2:9).

He's the surgeon, cutting away the invisible stony heart (Ezekiel 36:26) which is so hateful and rebellious (Jeremiah 5:23) that God can't write His law on it. It is of such a nature, Jeremiah says, that our hearts are so deceitful that who can know it, but the Spirit which searches the heart (Jeremiah 17:9, 10a).

After this reminder, I got out of bed and wrote the

Needle in a Haystack

Lord a letter, as usual, in my diary:

"Dear Lord Jesus, if you want me to be baptized into You because You have not yet cut away this stony heart, I will obey, but I want this to be confirmed that it's You speaking to me. I ask it in Thy holy name. Amen."

A week later we had some unexpected visitors from Bethesda – Bob and Doris – that we had made friends with. The reason they came over was because the Lord had burdened them for Rubin's need to see the truth in water baptism for the circumcision of heart.

Bob began showing Rubin scripture after scripture. Rubin was doing the same, showing how God had already done the work in him. I just sat quietly on the couch not thinking anything of it. All of a sudden the thought came to me about that letter I wrote to the Lord, asking for confirmation.

I listened some more. I saw how Rubin was rejecting everything they said, and I was receiving it without saying a word. My heart started pounding like crazy. I just couldn't remain silent any longer.

I jumped up and said, "You didn't come to see Rubin. God sent you to me. A week ago I wrote a letter to the Lord asking Him concerning the very thing you're speaking to Rubin. I'm going to read the letter to you, so you'll see it for yourself."

They just couldn't get over it. I was so happy that I kissed Bob! And Doris has never forgotten it.

They came over on a Monday, and Wednesday night I was baptized. I asked Rubin if he too would be baptized with me, but he wouldn't hear of it. I told them that maybe I should wait so we could be baptized together.

Paula Agauas

Bob said, "No. We have to work out our salvation with fear and trembling" (Philippians 2:12). I agreed and arrangements were made for me to be baptized that Wednesday night.

Wednesday morning came, and I was getting excited. I tried to call the Wilsons to tell them to pick me up for the evening service but was unable to reach them. They didn't know what was transpiring.

It was after supper. I cleaned up the kitchen and decided to take a nap but was unable to do so. All kinds of thoughts went through my mind. "What will this one say and the other one? Rubin doesn't even want to see me being baptized for he doesn't see God in it..."

I got real good and angry and said, "I don't care if the whole world is against me as long as I have God!" I jumped off the bed and began to dress for church. The telephone rang at the same time, and it was the Wilsons asking if I was going to go to church with them. Of course they were delighted to hear I planned going to church that night.

Rev. James Beall interviewed me that night. I told him how I heard myself asking God to circumcise my heart, and so on.

He said, "Who am I to go against the Holy Ghost?"

As I was walking into the baptistery, I knew without a shadow of a doubt that Jesus Christ would perform the operation of circumcision on my heart. But He had to use a vessel of His choosing to perform this act, and it was through Rev. Harry Beall.

There was a peace in that water. Only God's presence could have created that atmosphere. The congregation sang, 'Everybody ought to know who Jesus is.'

Needle in a Haystack

Not realizing it, I was singing solo.

Everybody ought to know

Everybody ought to know

Everybody ought to know

Who Jesus is.

He's the Lily of the Valley

He's the Bright and Morning Star

He's the Fairest of Ten Thousand

Everybody ought to know

After I was immersed, the first thing that came out of my mouth was, "I'm free, I'm free!" (John 8:32). Praise the Lord, He did set me free to worship Him in spirit and in truth (John 4:23).

I remember how I used to sing love songs, but after I came to know the Lord of lords and King of kings (Revelation 17:14) and who it is that truly loves me, I couldn't help myself. I sang unto Him day and night. Yes, even in my sleep. Praise God, I haven't stopped singing.

One afternoon as I was in the kitchen, Nathan had his little boyfriend over. As they were playing, Gary said to him, "My mom sings love songs."

And Nathan said, "But my mom sings love songs to Jesus all the time, not like your mom."

This was the first time that it really dawned on me that Nathan knew the difference. I had never told him about my experience, especially about Jesus Christ the Baptizer. He was only about six years old and yet so sensitive to the things of God.

One time I was asked to go to a prayer meeting at a Presbyterian church in the evening to speak to them. Of course Rubin and I took Nathan along. He sat there with his mouth wide open.

As we were on the way home, Nathan said to me, "All those bedtime stories you've been telling me, about this little girl and how Jesus watched over her, well, it's you. You were that little girl."

I said, "What makes you think it's me?"

"I remember some of the things you said at the prayer meeting. They were the same you told me," he answered. I had no alternative but to confess.

Not too long after God had done this work in me in the water of baptism, God also revealed Himself to Rubin as the Baptizer. He was baptized for the circumcision of heart and was filled with the Holy Ghost in the same evening. So now we were both in the New Covenant together.

After that we were received into the fellowship of Bethesda Missionary Temple where God was to root us in Him by laying the true foundation stones as recorded in Hebrews 6:1, 2 and 1 Timothy 4:14.

God opened a door and called us into a school of the Holy Spirit (Ministers Candidate School). Every Monday for three years, we attended this school. The second year the truth came to us that we were to be confirmed, so we enrolled in catechism (a study of the Bible). In the same year, the bonds of the presbytery were laid on us, and God confirmed to our hearts the ministry and gifts we were to have in functioning as members of His body.

Needle in a Haystack

Following are the people and their prophecies given:

Brother James Beall: *For the Word of God declares that I will bring My own by a way that they know not. I will bring them in a strange way, and I will bring them by a strange path. For even this night in God, you find the Lord doing for you what you declared would never be done. For the Lord doth fashion a vessel. Who hath been the instructor of the Lord, or who hath given Him wisdom? Ah, the Lord hath called thee to bring thee to this hour, to set thee apart, to ground thee and settle thee and to make thee as a pillar in the household of God, to let thy roots go down deep that thy life might be fruitful indeed. And that the blessing of God might be your portion. Turn not to the right hand or to the left hand, saith the Lord, and I will yet lead thee by a way that thou knowest not. For I shall perform in you my purposes, saith the Lord. The eyes of your understanding shall be enlightened, and teachers and instructors in righteousness indeed shall thou be. For the Lord shall open the eyes of your understanding. The Word of the Lord shall be illuminated unto thee, and it shall be as a new day of understanding and witness. And the wellsprings of prophecy shall well up within thee, and the word of the Lord shall be sounded as a blown trumpet in the midst of Zion. Hallelujah! Receive ye this gift of the Lord thy God. Hallelujah!*

Paula Agauas

Sister Patricia Gruits: *For the gift of faith and the gift of discerning of spirits doth the Lord grant unto thee. And thou shalt know the mind of God, and thou shalt prophesy that word. Yea, thou shalt even teach that word to those that know not the way. And thou shalt be astonished at the way that the Lord shalt use thee. Be willing to be led by the Lord. Give thyself up to be led of Him, and He shall lead thee in a plain path. A path where there shall be no doubt in thy mind, but that thou art walking in the path that He hath ordained for thee. Be thou careful, warneth the Lord, for when thou art confused and thou knowest not what the right path is, know that it is the devil himself that is trying to deceive thee and confuse thee and bring thee into error. For the Lord's voice is a clear voice, and His path is a clear path. And He shall show it to thee, and thou shalt never doubt that thou hast found the way of the Lord.*

Brother Harry Beall: *For surely thou hast found the well, yea, even thou hast found this great water of God. For He has taken thee from dryness, taken thee from the barren wilderness, and He has led thee even unto the streams of living water that flow from the throne of God. Yea, and thou shalt be given life and shalt pour out a drink to the cattle of the Lord. Yea, thou shalt pour out a drink of living water, for thou hast found the source of life, even the water of the living God. Yea, fear not. Fear not to drench thyself and thy bucket in this water. Fear not to take it up and dispense it, saith the Lord, for this is what thou hast looked for. This is what thine heart has longed to find. Yea, and thou hast found it, saith the Lord. He shall give thee a great desire wherewith thou shalt see the thirsty given drink.*

Needle in a Haystack

Brother Jim: *I see Rubin being given an appetite for the Word of the Lord as food. Like a man who hasn't been hungry for a long time, but suddenly it tastes so good... that it tastes like honey in his mouth. Ah, it tastes like bread indeed. I can almost see him running to share it. Running here and running there to tell the Word of the Lord that is like honey on his tongue and bread that satisfies his hungry soul. Hallelujah, be unto Thy name. So let it be, Lord. So let it be. Filled with the Word, Lord, with the taste of the Word of God indeed. Hallelujah.*

Brother Elton Weatherly: *I believe I see our sister...God anointing a knowledge she already has of languages, and she'll minister in these different languages. God will anoint that word, even in His name, Amen.*

Prayer – Brother Manly Higgins: *Father, we realize they haven't chosen Thee, but Thou hast chosen them and ordained them. Grant that they may bring forth fruit that their fruit might remain. From this very hour, may they be conscious of Thy plantation, that they shall be rooted and grounded in Thee. Established and strengthened into the calling wherewith Thou hast called them this hour. We charge them this night to be faithful into this ordination which Thou art calling them into, Lord, that they may bring forth fruit unto righteousness. For Thy glory and honor and praise we ask it. Amen.*

Having two boys of an age that baby sitters were needed, attending school wasn't easy. When we received an invitation to Ministers Candidate School, the first thing that came to our minds was a baby sitter. With Rubin not working at a paying job, it was impossible. The only thing for us to do was to commit the whole thing to God. We prayed. If it was of God, there is no doubt that He'd have a baby sitter in store for us.

After we left it in His hands, God did inform us who the baby sitter was to be. I called her up at work and told her that we were asked to come into the Ministers Candidate School. I asked if she would be willing to baby sit for us.

The first thing she said was, "Of course, I'd love to." We told her that we wouldn't be able to pay her. She just said, "I know," and that was it.

So God hired Eleanor Albert to be our baby sitter every Monday for three years, and she received her pay from Him privately. She was a very faithful steward and servant indeed.

Talking about baby sitters, one Thursday evening on catechism night, Eleanor was unable to baby sit. Nathan was nine at that time. So I said to Rubin, "Nathan will sit. If God watched over me, and I had no roof over my head, why should we worry? He can baby sit with Joey."

Rubin agreed. I informed Nathan of his job. He said he'd do it. Just as we were about to leave, he called me to his bed and said, "What am I going to do if I'm afraid?"

I said, "If this happens, just call on Jesus, and you'll be OK."

We were in class that first night, and I had peace about it for a little while. All of a sudden I knew that

Needle in a Haystack

Nathan was afraid. So I asked God to bring to his remembrance my instructions. After that I had peace.

We came home, and the boys were asleep. In the morning I asked Nathan if he had any trouble falling asleep.

He said, "After you left I was fine. I was about to go to sleep when this terrible fear came over me. I covered my head with my blanket, afraid to look out, when all of a sudden I remembered. I called on Jesus to help me, and it was like you said. He did help me. I took the cover off my head, had no fear, and I fell asleep. I will baby sit for you every Thursday."

Not long after this experience, God filled him with the Holy Ghost. It happened while I was vacuuming and praising God, singing in the Spirit, not realizing that Nathan was not only playing but also listening.

He came and asked if he too could sing as I did. He took me by surprise for a second. I didn't know what to answer him. Then I said, "You really mean it?"

He said, "Yes."

I sat down on the chair, had him kneel and lay his head on my lap. I asked God to grant unto him his desire. Before I knew it, he was anointed by the Holy Spirit, and he spoke in a beautiful heavenly language.

His eyes were like diamonds, just sparkling. I had the most beautiful child in the world in front of me! A few days later he received revelation about what it is to be buried into Christ, and he wanted his heart circumcised. He was real hurt when we told him that he'd have to wait until he went through the catechism class and then be baptized and confirmed as it is in Christ Jesus.

As you can see, our lives were full of excitement.

Paula Agauas

There was no time to be bored.

After all this, I began to feel kind of tired. We went to a wedding one Saturday. As I was standing in the lobby, I got dizzy and fainted. When I awoke I just couldn't understand my actions. A few nights later I dreamed that I had a third boy, and said, "Now I have a Nathan, a Joseph and a David." It was so real that, when I awakened, I was disappointed it was just a dream.

One month went by. I finally decided to have a checkup. Rubin was sure that I was going to have a baby, but I was sure that I wasn't. I just couldn't, not when things were the way they were. Rubin wasn't working, and we had no money to buy anything. I had given all our baby clothes away knowing for sure that I was through having babies. All kinds of things came to my mind.

The nurse called me in, and Dr. Weisberg examined me but was unable to tell a thing. Of course, I reassured him that I wasn't pregnant. But to make sure, he had to take a urine specimen and told me to sit in the waiting room for 10 minutes. In 10 minutes the nurse called me and said, "Mrs. Agauas, the test shows positive."

I said, "What's positive?"

"Don't you know, Mrs. Agauas?" she said. "You're going to have a baby."

I just couldn't believe it! I didn't want a baby. I was called into the office to see the doctor again. As I was sitting there I could hardly control myself. Every nerve in my body was irritated.

Until I came to Bethesda and met Helen, I never knew or heard of retarded children. I quite often

Needle in a Haystack

remarked to Helen who had a retarded boy, "How happy I am that I never had seen this before I had my boys. I would've been scared stiff to become pregnant."

All these things came into my mind. All of a sudden I became very quiet, and these words came to me. "I am the Lord that openeth the womb, and I am the One that closeth the womb."

All the anxiety left me. Instead, it was replaced with such a joy that I could've jumped to the ceiling. With the knowledge that this baby was of the Lord, I wasn't to be afraid. When the doctor came in he found me a different person, but he looked worried.

I asked him, "What's the matter?"

He said, "You know you're pregnant. This is really your fourth pregnancy, and your being RH negative makes it not very good. You had a miscarriage in your fourth month after Nathan was three years old. Remember? I'll have to watch you very closely, and you'll have to be very careful."

If I hadn't heard what I did from my first Physician, Jesus, I would've been scared stiff of the second one. All the fears I had, he would have confirmed. What a God we have. Praise His holy name.

The days and weeks went by. Some were good and some bad. One morning as I was walking up from the basement, this thought came to me. "You shall have a perfect child."

I was in the fifth month, and I hardly felt a baby. When I was in my seventh month I hardly showed. I told a lady that I often talked to in the church lobby that I was going to have a baby. She looked at me and wasn't joking when she said, "You aren't pregnant. If you are, it's probably a tumor." I assured her, but she didn't believe me.

After that I began thinking in that area, but the word came back to me, "You shall have a perfect baby." From the beginning to the time I entered the hospital, I was kept by the Word of God.

The Ministers Candidate School planned a surprise baby shower for me two weeks before I was due. Personally, I never liked baby showers before the baby was born. Of course, I didn't know a thing about it, but I surprised them instead.

The baby came Sunday morning, and the shower was planned for the following Monday. Rubin called me Tuesday morning telling me about it, and how he had to be the embarrassed recipient of the baby gifts. Of course, they had mercy on him and had him open only a few gifts. As for the rest, he decided to bring a few each day to the hospital. So every day for eight days I had gifts to open.

The reason I stayed that long in the hospital was because of the terrible headaches I had. They continued for five weeks. The Wilsons cared for me and the family all that time, without our having to pay them a penny. They did it all as unto the Lord. I can say that they were our spiritual parents. The Word of God declares, "God shows no partiality." The Wilsons were a perfect example of it. No matter whom they would have over to their house, they would entertain them royally.

Because of them we met quite a few nice people. One of them was Bernice Vedane from Pontiac, Michigan, a school teacher. She, too, became part of us. I would say she was like an older, protective sister. She understood me in every respect.

For two summers she took us out to Forester, Michigan, where she had a house right on Lake Huron.

Needle in a Haystack

At that time Joseph was one year old and Nathan, six. She did everything for us so I could have the proper rest. I felt as if God sent her down from heaven to serve us in such a royal way.

The children, Rubin and I had a heavenly time. We were hoping that this could go on every summer. So was Bernice, but she was a widow. Not having a husband to look after the place, she had to sell it. It didn't take long before it was sold.

One morning I received a call from her telling me that she was going to give me her 1961 Ford. That is, if I wanted it. I couldn't believe my ears! She had to repeat herself. The only thing that worried her was that it had a standard shift. I had never learned to use it, but it would just take two lessons for me to learn, she said. I took it out by myself after one lesson.

She told me afterward that God had burdened her for me, that I needed a new car for the one I was driving wasn't safe. She told the Lord if He sent her a buyer for that property, she'd give me the car. She not only gave me the car, but, since it was my birthday, it had a ribbon on it.

She also presented me with a Duncan-Phyfe, five-piece dining room set. In addition, she gave me a chest and desk combination. Who can tell me that He is not the Lord that provideth (Genesis 22:13)?

Her name became Mrs. Harold Smock when she married her former brother-in-law after she retired from teaching. They moved to Sarasota, Florida. A few years later her husband became very ill and died, and she moved back to Michigan. Sometime later, she had a stroke and went to be with the Lord.

Paula Agauas

Chapter 13
A Perfect Child

A third son was born to us, just as in the dream. We named him David Michael Agauas. We had no choice, since he was already named before his birth. I even had the privilege and experience of knowing how a mother feels by breast-feeding a child. This way proved wonderful for four months, and then Mother Nature cut off the supply.

As he was inactive when I carried him, so was he slow in developing. He was eight months old and didn't know how to hold his own bottle or reach out his hand if anything was being given to him. But I just loved him! It seems that the love I had for him took away my fears and anxieties.

One Sunday morning when I took him to the church nursery, this sweet lady said to me, "You know, Mrs. Agauas, David lies on his back and doesn't know how to turn over. And his legs look crooked." I just looked at her as if she wasn't even talking to me.

He had turned 16 months old already but was very slow in walking. Then I began to think. One morning as I was in the kitchen with David sitting in the high chair, I began to get angry, seemingly for no reason. I remembered what God said to me – that he would be a perfect child.

But looking at the child I saw no perfection. Something was not developing right. I was angry with God and said, "You told me that he'd be perfect, that nothing would be wrong with him. Why is he so slow? His mentality is not that of a 16-month- old child."

Before I had a chance to say anything else, I began

Needle in a Haystack

to shake from head to toe. My hands burned like fire. As I looked at them, this word came to me. "I am the Resurrection."

I said, "Yes, Lord, You are the Resurrection," as if I never had heard of it before. While I was still looking at my hands, I was directed to lay them on David's head and said, "In Jesus' mighty name, I command every brain cell to be restored and develop as it was meant to be, that every part of this body will function right!"

I took my hands off of his head not fully realizing what had taken place. I just praised God for revealing Himself to me as the very Resurrection and completely forgot about David.

I would have had to be blind not to acknowledge what was happening. David got himself down from the high chair and started walking as though he had walked for six months. He looked and responded in every way like God said he would.

God had allowed this to happen that I might know Him as the Resurrection. God not only resurrected the child, but resurrected the whole household. He literally opened the windows of heaven.

After seven years of unemployment, I was getting very irritable having Rubin around me. One morning as I was making the bed, I told the Lord that it was about time that Rubin got a job and got out of my hair. I was becoming a cripple in my own kitchen with Rubin wanting to tell me how to boil water.

As I was in this state of mind, the telephone rang. It was a friend, John, asking for Rubin. He said to me, "Mr. Gruits wants him to come to the church press for there is some work for him."

I asked him, "How did you know what I was just

Paula Agauas

telling God?"

He said, "What?"

Rubin was out, probably visiting with the Wilsons, when the call came. When he came home, I informed him about the telephone call. He was ecstatic about it and couldn't wait to get there. Little did I realize that he, too, not knowing what to do with himself anymore, felt as I did. Yet, God said that He will not suffer us to be tempted above that we are able to bear (1 Corinthians 10:13).

Of course Rubin did whatever work there was to be done without being particular. A few months later, John took him to see a house that was for rent in Warren. Rubin called, told me about a seven-room place that we were going to move into and asked me to come and look at it.

I called Bernice, and she went with us. We then rented a house on Packard Street in Warren, Michigan. It was like a palace in contrast to the five-room flat we had.

Rubin enrolled in a class to learn how not to be dependent as much on his sight, but more by touch which gave him more confidence. Afterward, the blind man made arrangements with G.M. for an interview for a job. He was hired as a line inspector because of his special ability he had learned by touch.

After six months Social Security Disability decided he was capable of working. Due to his new ability on the job, they had no need to send him further disability checks.

Nathan turned 12 and was confirmed. We were able to give him a confirmation party – a true "Bar-Mitzvah." A week later we had cousins over from New

109

Needle in a Haystack

York. We were so happy that we had room for them.

Two years later my sister's daughter, Helen, came to visit us from Israel. When I last saw her, she was in Germany and was then only six months old. Now she was 21 years old. I knew of her coming, but didn't know if her mother told her anything about my beliefs.

Unknown to me, she was well informed. She loved to hear everything, and God revealed Himself to her. Before she left, God met her in the waters of baptism, and we were able to worship Him under the same roof.

Before she returned to Israel, I gave her an English-Hebrew Bible. She was hesitant to take it with her for fear of her father. So I told her to give it to the Wilsons. The Wilsons first met Helen when they went with us to the airport to pick her up.

While she was still in the United States, the Wilsons had left for Israel and were staying in Netanya where Helen's parents live. Now the Wilsons minister to them, and they are very much loved by my family.

Helen felt better upon her arrival in Israel. She gave the Bible to the Wilsons and didn't say a word to her father about what had taken place in her life. I had instructed her not to unless God opened that door of utterance. Sure enough God did, and Helen told her father after awhile. But he instructed her not to tell a soul.

Paula Agauas

Chapter 14
Vacation by Grace

After a year, Eleanor Albert began to make plans to take a trip to Israel. She came over wishing I could go with her. I told her that it would be nice but impossible. I left it at that. I had a desire to visit Israel for 21 years in order to see my sisters and their families. But I knew that it would be impossible due to our lack of money. And who would take care of the family with David being 3 ½ years old?

One afternoon I was resting. I had my eyes shut, just about to doze off. This word kept coming to me, "Without faith it is impossible to please God." It was as if I were hearing it for the first time. Yet I had heard it before. I knew it was a Biblical scripture.

So I asked Rubin if he knew where to find it, but he wasn't sure. I wondered why this word was coming to me now. I wasn't having any problems that would require this word. I tried to put it out of my thoughts, but was unsuccessful until I saw it for myself in the Bible in Hebrews 11:6. After that I received peace.

A few weeks went by. Eleanor came over to go with us to the 50th wedding anniversary of our pastor. As we were on the way, she expressed her wish that I come with her to Israel. Rubin asked her how much the trip would cost. She told us it would cost about $400 or $500 round trip including the fare from here to New York and back to Detroit.

Rubin then asked me, "Honey, why don't you go?"

I thought that was what I heard him say, so I said, "You really mean it?" I knew that he meant it. I was doing the driving, but it was as if I were flying. I knew

111

Needle in a Haystack

then and there that I was going to Israel. I had no doubt about it. Eleanor was just beside herself with joy when I told her.

After coming home and going to bed, I found myself just lying there and not being able to sleep. You see, I came down to earth, and all that excitement turned into anxiety and worry about what I was going to do for money? I didn't have it. Who was going to drive Rubin to work for two weeks while I was gone? Who was going to take care of them, especially David? As far as I was concerned, the trip was off!

I tried to go to sleep but was unable to because of all these worries. Then my spirit was eased, and this word came to my remembrance. "Without faith it is impossible to please God."

Of course, God gave me this word before. I couldn't for the life of me understand why. But now it was clarified as to why He needed to give me that kind of a word. I was even offended at Him. Why? Haven't I been living by faith all this time? Didn't I have a right to think that way? Of course. Yes, and so do many others, but the word does declare that *"the heart of man is deceitful and desperately wicked, who knows it, but the Spirit who searches the heart* (Jeremiah 17:9, 10).*"

After God brought back the word to me in such force, that word was not just a word anymore but a search light in my own heart. I could've just buried myself alive but praise God for the power of the blood.

After I ate of the word and digested it, I had no more trouble going to sleep. I awakened with Rubin's telephone call, telling me to pick him up from work. The first thing he said was, "I have it all worked out. The two weeks' vacation I'm supposed to get in July, I'll take it the two weeks in September that you're gone. That

112

Paula Agauas

way, we'll have no problems."

Now why didn't I think of that? Then I asked him, "What are you going to do about the money?"

He said, "I'll take a loan from the bank. Our credit is good, you know."

Everything he said seemed right except for one thing – borrowing from the bank. I felt a check. I couldn't see paying interest on that money and felt this move just couldn't be of God. I told him my feelings and left it.

I had the passport pictures taken and applied for a passport which arrived in three weeks. The only thing missing was the ticket. I called Eleanor to find out when I would need to give her the $300 for the deposit so Rubin would know how much to borrow from the bank.

She said, "I'll lend you the money for this trip. Why pay interest? You just pay me back as you can." That's all I had to hear. The way was cleared.

Until then, I hadn't informed my sister of my plans to come. So I wrote her an airmail letter with much excitement. Then I was really on my way, making full preparation for that God-given trip.

On September 7, 1970, I was on my way to Israel on El-Al Airlines. We were flying during the hijackings, but we had peace knowing that the trip was of the Lord. We were three hours late arriving in Tel-Aviv, but it was all worth it. The Wilsons brought my two sisters, Helen and David, her brother. Not seeing them for 22 years, we had quite a reunion.

It was midnight when we arrived in Nadine. It only took a half hour from Tel-Aviv. My brother-in-law, Helen's father, was still up. I guess he had expected to

Needle in a Haystack

see a great change in me for he kept saying as he was hugging me, "The same Paula. We thank God for the same, happy Paula." In his eyes, I even looked as young as when he last saw me 22 years ago when I was 15 years old.

Eleanor and I were very tired, and we all went to sleep. We were awakened by someone beating on a carpet outside a window at 4:00 a.m. The sun was already out. My sister's place on the fourth floor had no screens in the windows, just shutters, and yet no flies came in. The sky was so very clear. I felt as if the whole world and its problems were behind me, and I was taken up into a completely new atmosphere.

The morning started with my brother-in-law leaving for work at 5:00 a.m., Helen at 8:00 a.m. for work and David for school. It was his last year in high school. David's whole personality was just like Nathan's.

Eleanor and I had breakfast. Then we asked Genia, my sister, to take us down for a walk. The air was just breathtaking. While in the U.S. most of the flowers had lost their bloom, there it was just like spring. The weather was like mid-summer here. I went swimming in the Mediterranean Sea. It was my first experience swimming in salty water. After I got out I couldn't wait to go home and take a shower for I was full of salt.

I also went swimming at a place called 'Sachna.' There the water was so soft that I was scared stiff to let myself go into it. I just sat myself down on a rock with my feet in it, and the little fish nibbled at my toes.

The scenery was just beautiful. It reminded me of the story in the Bible when Moses was found in the basket by the princess, the daughter of Pharaoh, where she and her maidens were swimming (Exodus 2:5). This

Paula Agauas

was how I visualized it as I was sitting there, watching some of the swimmers jumping off the high cliffs into that warm soapy-like water.

I also arrived just in time for my older sister's grandson's Pinene Ben (Dedication to God). It was a beautiful celebration. My older sister's boy's name was also Nathan, after our father. He married a very nice girl. She prepared a beautiful dinner the first Saturday we were there and was full of hospitality. In fact, every place we were taken by my sisters, the first thing we were offered was food. And you just had to eat it.

The Wilsons took us around to all the places we wanted to see. And by the way, money was no problem for me.

After we came back from the walk that first day, we had lunch and took a nap. While Eleanor and I were napping, my two sisters had to attend to some business in Tel-Aviv. When we awakened, they were already back.

They were full of excitement, telling me, "We've been waiting for eight years for this money to be released to us from the German government claims. Because you're such a miracle, God had to send you before we could get that money."

I remembered about nine years ago, they did send me some papers to sign concerning that money, but I didn't want any part of it. I thought to myself, "Let them have it," and never gave it another thought.

I arrived in Israel, and that money was following me. The very next day my share of 600 pounds was handed to me by my sisters. I wanted them to have it, but they wouldn't hear of it.

I felt like Cinderella for two weeks. I didn't have to

Needle in a Haystack

count my pennies. I had money for gifts to bring home and gifts for the family and friends. The spending money of $200 which I had brought with me, I didn't have to touch. I brought it all back.

Only my Lord could've planned this trip so perfectly for me. He even had an Arab take Rubin and me, with the boys, to Detroit Metro Airport, singing praises to God on the way. When I arrived from Israel, he brought my family to pick me up from the airport. So in God there is no Jew or Gentile – no Jew or Arab – but we are all one in Christ Jesus (Galatians 3:28).

After two weeks being away from the children, it was mighty good to see them again, even though it seemed like I forgot I had a family while I was in Israel. I felt very single. Rubin was very happy to see me return, for he had a few scares with the hijackings that were going on.

Everything worked for good, for I had a new husband, full of appreciation. God knows from the beginning to the end what is good for an individual.

Paula Agauas

Chapter 15
A Place for Us

Before I went to Israel, Rubin and I were talking about looking for another place to live, for we were being tried by our landlords to the utmost. For example, they called us up on the telephone one evening and gave us two weeks' notice that they were raising our rent $40. They stated that if we didn't like it, we'd just have to move.

Yet we know that God allowed this too. Of course, we weren't prepared for an extra $40 in two weeks. A sister in the Lord handed me an envelope containing $20 toward that rent. I had told her about it, but with no intention of getting any help from her. She said it wasn't her idea. It was her friend's idea to give us $10, and she added the other $10.

That money to me was not just from them, but a sign from God that He'd provide. I had peace about it to the point that I was able to pray for the landlords and not despise their actions.

After these landlords, the thought of renting again made me sick. Deep down in my heart I knew that when we moved from this place, it would be the last place we were going to rent.

The winter months were over, and Memorial Day weekend came. The weather was very nice. Rubin was sleeping for he worked nights. I went over to our Egyptian neighbors who had moved next door to us while I was in Israel. I asked if they would like to go to Toepfer Park. She asked her husband, Sabry, and he thought it was a good idea.

As we were sitting in the park talking, Isis said,

117

Needle in a Haystack

"Paula, come. Let's take a ride in front of the park on MacArthur. There's a house that my friend wants to buy. I want you to look at it."

I said, "OK." We got the children together and went to see that house. As we stopped, I saw this real estate sign. So I said, "Isis, you can't go into this house. You have to make an appointment."

Then she said, "Why don't you buy this house? It has everything you want in it – four bedrooms, a basement, garage and so on."

I said, "Isis, you are crazy! I could never afford this house."

She got out of the car and ran to ring the bell. Sure enough, this man came out and motioned to us to come in. We had no choice. When I entered the front room and looked in, I just couldn't believe my eyes. As I walked through the house, especially when I saw the same hair spray that I was using standing on the vanity, I then had no doubt of the house not being ours.

It was a bungalow house, the kind I had been wanting since we've been married – 18 years. The house was owned by a retired couple. They were selling it so they could buy a trailer in Florida. I asked them, "How much money do you want for a down payment?"

They said, "Nothing, just a closing cost for it's being sold on an FHA mortgage." I couldn't believe my ears. He, Mr. Van Huly, told me to just go over to this real estate office and give them a deposit on the house.

I went home, and Rubin was still asleep. When he woke up he wasn't in too good a mood. So I just didn't mention it to him. The following morning, after I picked him up from work, I asked him, "Would you like to see this house that I looked at yesterday?"

Paula Agauas

He said, "Yes."

I took him there. He didn't even have to see the inside. He wanted to run over and put a deposit on that house. Of course, he looked through it. Mr. Van Huly told us that he had already called the real estate office and informed them that we were interested. That day we knew the house was ours.

After talking to the agent and having him tell us our chances, we had a few doubts. So I said, "You better pray with us," and we left. As I walked out of there, I thought to myself, "We didn't yet get a positive word from God concerning this house."

We got in the car, and as I was driving this word came to me, "I am the Lord that rules in men's affairs." I said, "Rubin, I got a word concerning the house."

He said, "What is it?" I told him, and he said, "The house is ours."

On July 29, 1971, we signed papers, and the house was ours. In the first week of September we occupied it. It was exactly one year before that date that God sent me to Israel.

Yes, without faith it is impossible to please Him, for He is a rewarder of them that diligently seek Him (Hebrews 11:6). We didn't even have to take the children out of school, because we were still in the same district.

We are situated across from a park and only five minutes from church. After 19 years of marriage, not knowing what it would be like not having someone living over you or under you, we are now experiencing what it feels like to live in a private dwelling. What a palace!

This earthly dwelling place that the Lord has supplied is nothing in comparison to the vision He gave

Needle in a Haystack

me in my night's sleep about 12 ½ years ago. I was on a ship, and in it were many compartments filled with people. But something happened to it, and we were unable to go on.

I jumped off and proceeded to swim toward the shore for help, but I was running out of strength as the waves grew too big for me to swim over. From nowhere, I suddenly had someone on each side of me, helping me along as if I were carried over the waves. In a little while they let go of me. I was able to swim on my own with them talking to me. Of course, I told them why I was swimming to this shore.

We reached the shore, and what did I see but houses with their doors wide open. I said to them, "It's night, and the people are asleep. Why don't they shut their doors?"

They said, "Why, there are no thieves here nor anyone to fear, for everyone loves one another."

The flowers in front of the houses were just breathtaking. Then, in front of us, I saw lambs, lions and all kinds of animals together. I asked, "How can this be?"

As I questioned, a lamb came up to me and greeted me. I said to the ones on each side of me, "I don't want to go back. It's so peaceful here. The water is so fresh, and it smells so good. I want to live here forever."

They answered me and said, "Did you forget why you came here? The people on that boat depend on you to save them. Now, go back to them, for they need you. After you've done the job, you'll come back."

The only comment I can make about this is what the Word of God declares: *"The just shall live by faith (Romans 1:17)."*

About the Author

Rubin and Paula were blessed with three sons – Nathan, Joseph and David – and four grandchildren – Daniel, Hannah, Stephen and Kristin. All of them have accepted Jesus, the Messiah.

Paula was married for 55 years before God took her husband home.

The prophecy from God that Angie's mother, the fortune teller, spoke over Paula so many years ago was fulfilled: The new country (USA) will be very good to her.

Many people have come to know the truth about the living God through her testimonies. God inspired her to write this book, Needle in a Haystack, to tell about *God of the Impossible.*

Paula currently resides in Warren, MI.

Made in the USA
Columbia, SC
23 October 2018